Homeschooling for Life
A Practical Guide for Emotional and Spiritual Growth

by Dr. Dale Simpson

HOMESCHOOLING FOR LIFE

Copyright © 2018 by Learning for Life Press. All rights reserved.
ISBN 978-0-9988624-3-9
Published by Learning for Life Press, Venice, Florida 34285

No portion of this book may be reproduced, in any form, without written permission from the publisher.

Printed in the United States of America

Table of Contents

Foreword i
Preface ii

Section 1: Parenting Power

Chapter 1: The Challenge to Raise Strong Children 2
Application 17

Chapter 2: Boundaries 19
Application 27

Chapter 3: Legacies to Leave Your Children ... 29
Application 36

Chapter 4: Successfully Navigating the Digital Life 39
Application 71

Chapter 5: Why Emotional Growth Takes So Long 73
Application 79

Chapter 6: Teaching Your Children to Fail 81
Application 87

Chapter 7: Helping the Troubled Child 89
Application 97

Chapter 8: A Call to Action 99
Application 105

Section 2: Marriage

Chapter 9: Marriage in a Paint Can 109
Application 115

Chapter 10: Marriage Roles or Rules? 117
Application 121

Chapter 11: Your Best Retirement Plan 123
Application 127

Section 3: Family

Chapter 12: For Dads Only 131
Application 136

Chapter 13: What to Do with Emotions 137
Application 144

Chapter 14: The Time Management Blues 147
Application 151

Chapter 15: Self-Esteem – Is It Selfishness? 153
Application 158

Chapter 16: Why Won't You Just Say Something?
.... 161
Application 165

Chapter 17: Are You Blocking Effective Communication? 171
Application 174

Section 4: Homeschooling and Life

Chapter 18: Is Giftedness Next to Godliness? 177
Application 182

Chapter 19: Homeschooling in the Real World....183
Application 193

Chapter 20: Are Your Standards Hurting You?....195
Application 200

Chapter 21: Balancing the Roles of Teacher and Parent..203
Application 211

Foreword

Dr. Simpson's perspective on parenting, marriage, and family life impacted me when I first discovered it years ago. And over these years, I have found it influencing me again and again. I have also witnessed firsthand the profound benefit of these techniques and principles as we have applied them in our family.

We believe that homeschooling is not just about the academic subjects but also about how to live. Dr. Simpson sees homeschooling this way as well, and the principles in this book have helped us through the ups and downs of family life. Families are not perfect and ours is no exception. But when you see emotional and spiritual growth occurring in your home, it gives you hope that you can go the distance.

Maybe we CAN home school for life. Maybe we CAN teach our children values and proper decision making (as well as math and science) with socks on the floor and dishes in the sink. The message of this book is that we surely can.

A Home School Parent

Preface

Knowledge comes from so many sources, making it impossible to identify many ideas and principles of living one absorbs. I have learned much over the last 37 years, with 27 of those years unfolding after the first edition of this book. So much has changed since the early 1990s and even now, the speed of change is ever increasing.

I have learned from homeschooling families in my local area and whom I met at state conventions year after year. I have benefited from those modern pioneers who went before us, forging a trail for home education's acceptance. Thanks also go to the patients who over the years, unknowingly taught me much as they courageously revealed themselves in therapy.

In ancient times, the role of prophet was to speak the truth boldly. Prophets often made those to whom they were speaking uncomfortable. Yet the message was that if they would face the truth, good things would come about. I was shocked to find out that each of our family members is in some way modern prophet. Living with them confronts us with both the pleasant and the unpleasant truths about ourselves. To my family, you have been bearers of the truth and I have been gratefully impacted by living with and knowing you.

Three areas of encouragement are woven through this book. First, homeschooling can be accomplished successfully and for as long as you wish to educate your children. Second, burnout is not inevitable, although it can result if the proper expectations and elements are not in place. Third, homeschooling is for life. It is about how to live successfully, learning from many sources, keeping relationships at the heart of our family.

"Thank you's" are in order to the many helpful and capable people who contributed to this book, including Patti Pearson and Joanna Robinson. Also, note that a number of the chapters are modified articles originally published in Homeschooling Today® Magazine through my column *Inside the Family*.

Special thanks go out to Todd Wilson, 'The FamilyMan' for granting permission to use his cartoons found in this book. They were taken from The Official Book of Homeschooling Cartoons. You can purchase his books at www.thesmilinghomeschooler.com or at our website, www.learningforlifepress.com.

As you read this book, may you find courage and freedom to be yourself, learn practical helps, and realize that you can be a family that is Homeschooling for Life.

The pronouns "he" or "him" are frequently used as generic terms meaning male or female to avoid cumbersome language.

Dale Simpson

Introduction

Whether you're a first-time homeschooler or a veteran, Homeschooling for Life, A Practical Guide for Emotional and Spiritual Growth, provides helpful tools and sound advice for meeting the needs of the child, parent and home school family. In this breakthrough book, author Dale Simpson shares his decades of wisdom and experience as a psychologist, noted educator, and home school father. He gives you insights that, when applied, will make family life more fulfilling, rewarding, enjoyable and fun filled.

The title of the book, Homeschooling for Life, plays off two meanings of the phrase. The first is that the home school lifestyle is really about life, relationships, and something much larger than education. The second meaning comes from one of Dr. Simpson's central reasons in writing the book: *to support families so they can go the distance in home education.*

With gentle encouragement, keen insights, practical applications, and thought-provoking questions, Homeschooling for Life equips you to be more of the parent you want to be. Packed with specific tools and techniques, you will learn skills that are useful until your last child is out the door; and then it's on to the grandchildren!

Learn how to:

- Effectively communicate
- Nourish your marriage, the foundation of the family system
- Deal with a challenged child
- Fight perfectionism and prevent burnout
- Teach your children self-control that is truly inside them
- Avoid power struggles and keep parenting fun

And so much more to make your homeschooling and your family a success.

Homeschooling for Life is like having your own psychological coach available anytime; an expert who can bring about life-changing experiences for your home school family.

Section 1: Parenting Power

Dr. Dale Simpson

Chapter 1: The Challenge to Raise Strong Children

If you cause one of these little ones to stumble, you might as well be thrown in the ocean with a huge rock hung around your neck.

-Jesus

Carol was the perfect teenager. She sang in the choir, led the honor society, and dressed modestly when others around her did not. She even grew up to be a minister's wife with several children. Her parents were proud. But one day, Carol left a note for her husband and kids saying that she was leaving them all to make a new life with the next-door neighbor, who left his wife and kids to be with Carol.

Her parents were devastated, the church congregation was astounded, and her husband was crushed. What happened to Carol? She had seemed to be doing so well, but as time so clearly showed, she was not able to consistently make wise choices throughout her life. She seemed to be leading an exemplary life, but in the end, she crashed in moral ruin.

One of the biggest challenges facing parents today is raising children who can make tough choices. This world needs children, who, when they become adults, can make choices that are healthy and wise. These choices may go against the grain of today's society and morality, but such choices will ultimately lead to a satisfying life. We want long-term happiness for our children, rather than something fleeting that masquerades as happiness. The ability to choose wisely will lead to a satisfying and contented life.

How do we parents strengthen our children's ability to make decisions in a world often hostile to our values? As we see in Carol's case, just teaching them to believe the right thing is not enough to ensure they will actually make the right choices

There are many competing priorities — our own impulses, someone else urgently telling us to do something, or perhaps even some unethical temptation, born of a dishonest business environment. We usually know what the right choice is, but living has to be more than just knowing right from wrong. Our children face similar challenges, which become more difficult as they grow older, with higher stakes. Exposing our children from an early age to the concept of taking responsibility for their actions will ultimately yield strong decision-makers who understand, through experience, that they are the captains of their little decision-making ships. They are the ones primarily responsible for their destiny.

What if you gave your children their choice of a curfew? Or allowed them to decide whether or not to pick up their clothes or clean their rooms? What if you let them decide whether or not to use drugs or alcohol?

"Letting" your children choose probably sounds permissive. But are you really giving up anything by acknowledging that children do choose? You're not going to be with them every minute of their lives. You won't be on that date, in that business environment, or in that marriage. So, how do you strengthen your child's ability to make solid moral choices? You have a central task - to guide them so they learn responsibility by facing their challenges and decisions. Giving them freedom within limits, then providing appropriate consequences in the face of their choices is the best way for strengthening their moral compass, while helping them learn.

Peter hits a ball through his neighbor's window and then asks his father to apologize to the neighbor for him. The father's first tendency might be to talk to the neighbor because he can explain things better than his twelve- year-old. If the father did that, he would be stealing something important from his child. The child needs to face up to his actions, and if he doesn't learn this over a broken window now, he'll avoid taking responsibility in a tougher situation later. This can be done straightforwardly and without shaming the child.

So, as a loving parent, Peter's father stands behind him as Peter apologizes to the neighbor. And when it comes time to pay for the window, the father will ask Peter how he wants to solve that problem, and may even help Peter find a way to earn some money.

Remember, if it's an eight-year-old child and a $500 window, it may take him two lifetimes of allowances to pay for it. This is where you need to use your ability to decide on a readily attainable and logical solution. Perhaps it would be best to let him pay fifty cents a week out of his allowance for a certain number of weeks, then you pay the rest. Let him feel some of the responsibility. Start now, before there are too many broken windows to deal with. Get him to think and develop that inner ability to make responsible choices.

Parenting Styles

We should, at all costs, avoid the three-R parenting styles: Ranting, Raving and Rescuing. All three are terribly ineffective ways to parent a child; for whatever occasional short-term gain, you will always experience long term losses. If you tell your child several times to do something and the child doesn't do it, the situation can escalate into angry yelling and screaming. Then he may start complaining and you might overreact with unreasonable discipline. "You're restricted for ten years!" "You can't leave the house for three months!" As parents, we paint ourselves into a corner and then have to back up and rescue the child from what we've threatened, ending up with the admonition, "Just don't do it again."

Ranting. Raving. Rescuing. These tactics produce kids who'll never learn how to make tough choices. We need to know how to say these things to our children: "Boy, you really have a dilemma. Man! I'm hurting for you. What are you going to do?" This leaves the problem resolution squarely where it belongs--with them.

Then there's the "No-Problem" approach of noted educator Jim Fay. Let's assume you've asked your seventeen-year-old at nine o'clock on Saturday morning to mow the lawn before he goes out with his buddies that night. Now it's 4:30 in the afternoon and he's running around, taking a shower, doing his hair, getting ready for a fun night. You ask him what he's going to do about the lawn and he replies that he'll get it done tomorrow or next week.

This is where the "No-Problem" technique comes in. "No problem, son!" you say. "I'll mow the lawn, but it will cost you twenty bucks," or, "No problem! I'll do it and just take the time spent cutting the grass from the time I was going to spend fixing your car next weekend."

Your options depend on what you have to work with. You trade one thing for another. If dad mows the lawn, the two hours have to be made up — whatever the son decides to do, "NO PROBLEM!" Just a note here — I usually don't trade one minute for one minute.

Dr. Dale Simpson

Since I have a job, my minutes cost more. Five minutes of my time doing his chore might cost a child twenty minutes of their time.

For younger children it could be something as simple as asking them to pick up their toys. "It's time to pick up the toys, Honey." The child looks up at you and says, "No, I don't want to." Tell the child, "No problem. You can pick them up or I can pick them up. But if I pick them up, I will put them in the Saturday basket and you will not get the toys back until next Saturday." It's the same principle.

You're probably thinking that the child will let you pick up every toy in the house. He doesn't care about his toys. Well, then, your problem is to figure out which toys or what things he cares about! Don't be afraid of giving them choices, choices within limits. Younger children especially need some fences or boundaries. "Free range" kids do not turn out as well as free range chickens!

Many of us are geared to give lectures. We're primed to give information. We lecture the children and they nod their heads and look like they're getting it. We're going on and on and they're nodding, "Uh-huh. Uh-huh," but it's not sinking in.

Instead of a lecture, they need a thinking kind of question. "Have you ever wondered what would happen if you ended up in jail?" "Have you ever wondered what would happen if you were in an automobile accident?" "Have you ever wondered what would happen if so and so ended up pregnant?" "Have you thought about the consequences?" Tell your child that maybe it's something they ought to think about. I'd then discuss out loud what consequences might ensue in each scenario. You need to talk about it and help them think it through.

We must help our children develop the "strong executive" inside who is comfortable making choices, who is used to judging the consequences and then deciding to live with them. Getting feedback about choices through consequences helps them change their behavior (this is called learning from experience.) They should be exposed to choices in direct proportion to their ability to make them. Somebody once called it the "v in the word love" in decision making. The bottom of the "V" is at birth and as you go up the widening "V" there is an increase in self-direction and freedom to make choices, all the way up to high school and leaving home at the top of the "V."

Unfortunately, families often function in reverse. Parents give kids too much free, unstructured latitude in the early years. Then as the kids get older, parents start clamping down out of fear by restricting their kids' freedom or decision-making capabilities. That's the wrong way. With this method, you will guarantee yourself power struggles with your teenager. It must be done correctly. The "V" of decision making must not be inverted.

Children need guidance concerning right and wrong, and the best way to do that is to live out our values in front of them. Proper values are caught, not taught. Children will observe how you treat laws and how you respond to laws and operate within limits. So, we must live out our values, not in a heavy-handed way, but sincerely integrated into our lifestyle.

Dr. Dale Simpson

Self-Control from the Inside

Difference between thinking and saying.

Another challenge for parents is teaching their children how to control impulses and emotions. The child must learn self-control in order to function effectively in society. Parents are also called to teach self-control because of God's instruction. Of course, the first line of teaching is to be sure that the parent shows self-control. Children will tend to learn the same level of self-control the parent maintains. Assuming that a parent is a model of self-control when a child is misbehaving, the challenge becomes finding a way to make each event a learning lesson.

If you are like me, my first impulse when I see misbehavior is to order it to stop. I immediately feel like barking out an order, since, after all, I'm one of the big guys and I set the rules. Besides, when kids are misbehaving, it's irritating. When I see or hear things that I don't particularly like, it feels good to bark out an order or a command. It can feel especially good on a day when I don't think anybody is listening to me. I can displace my anger by yelling out orders. My kids, of course, are a captive audience. It's hard for them to avoid my bad parenting.

The problem comes when we ask the question, "Does giving an order necessarily help them develop self-control over the long run?" I know that a command may help them show control at that moment. Kids are not stupid. They know if you are standing right there ready to blast them, they should stop. However, the parent's ultimate goal is not just simply to have their children act properly when they are in your midst. True self-control is control that occurs without the policeman standing there.

This inner control must begin with your external threats of unpleasantness ("If you touch that, I'll restrict you,") and move to their internal reference ("I want to steal this money, but it's wrong to do that.") The Christian perspective always calls us to look beyond behavior and look into the heart.

If our kids are going to show restraint in a world that disdains it, they must develop a strong function of choice within themselves. This "decision-maker" or "executive" part of their make-up needs to develop so it can stand in the face of external and internal pressures. We want the decision-making person strong so that he can withstand the demands and temptations of the world. If the executive is weak and is simply looking around for the policeman to determine if he should act correctly, he will never make it in a world full of freedoms. There just aren't enough policemen or inspectors in the world to make us all act properly. The belief is more important than the outward behavior. When a child misbehaves, he "believes" he knows better than the parent.

Parents in general, and Christian parents in particular, must be dedicated to strengthening the executive within our children, rather than weakening it. We must show them where the choices are in life and allow them to exercise their will.

How many times have we seen extremely well-behaved kids in controlled, highly religious families go on to college and simply lose control to drugs, sex and other forms of indulgence? This is frequently a sign that external controls were used but the executive was never fully developed in that child while in the home. Interestingly, one of the hopes of parents with strong willed children is that the strong will can be lovingly confronted and directed early on, making it easier for the child to resist peer pressure later on.

The Three-Question Method

How does the parent nurture internal control in the child without simply relying on external control? One simple, but highly effective technique is called the "Three Question Method." This method is not only good for kids but also prevents the parent from saying something unhelpful. Moreover, is it consistent with God's approach with us? He gives us seed to sow with, lets us sow to flesh or spirit, but He determines the harvest. (Gal 6:7-8)

Any time misbehavior is happening, you can help your children by going through a process of answering three questions. This takes more time initially than simply barking out an order, but in the course of the eighteen years you have to teach a child, this will help develop a solid internal center of control.

First, ask the child, "Honey, what are you doing right now?" This needs to be asked in as straightforward and businesslike tone as possible. The first week you implement this with your children, you will get responses like "I don't know" or statements that tell you what they are trying to do and not reflect on their actual behavior. For example, when they are nagging and whining, trying to talk you out of a limit, they may respond to, "What are you doing right now?" by saying, "I'm just trying to tell you something," to which the proper parental response is, "No, Honey, you are nagging and whining and arguing with me."

Give your children the room to understand what's going on when you implement this strategy. Usually it takes a week or so for kids to finally catch on. I tell teenagers that their parents are learning how to question them when they see misbehavior and helping them come to terms with it.

This first question has them face their behavior — to look at themselves, which is a biblical principle. Jesus said, "be sure to remove the log from your own eye before you start doing other things." Scripture is always calling us to honestly examine our own behavior and face anything that is ungodly. In fact, it is a wise man who can face himself; the fool minimizes and rationalizes. (Col 3:17)

The second question involves having the child reflect on the standard or template for behavior. This question asks, "What are you supposed to be doing?" Again, as you first implement this, kids will give you a range of responses including "I don't know." You must gently and firmly tell them, "What you are supposed to do is quit the arguing and get ready for bed," or whatever the proper response should be.

Having looked at their behavior, and then the template or standard for behavior, the third question calls the child to a choice. The parent then asks, "Now, what are you going to choose? It's up to you." The parent must understand that children make many mistakes and many bad choices in their young lives. In fact, in some ways we pray for many mistakes at the small level, when things have nickel-and-dime consequences. That is where they hopefully learn the lessons of life. If you are able to see mistaken choices not as terrible failures in the child or in your parenting, but as natural occurrences in the child's life, you will be able to openly allow the child to make a choice.

Again, during the first week, the child will usually balk at deciding and will often respond with "I don't know" when asked what they are going to choose. At this point, the loving parent simply says, "Well, if you keep doing that behavior after the next few seconds, I will take that as your choice to misbehave and I will discipline you. It's up to you.

The parent must have in his mind that if the child makes a bad choice, it is not the parent's problem. The parent's problem is explaining what the reasonable consequence for that misbehavior is and then following up on it. Following through with consequences can be time consuming and bothersome, but that's the price of parenting.

Something wonderful usually starts happening after the technique is established. You will find yourself asking a child in the middle of misbehavior "Honey, what are you doing right now?" and they will cast their eyes down and say "Okay," stopping the misbehavior. This is an important sign that they are doing steps two and three internally, which is exactly what you want. The extra time it has taken to teach them returns many times over because often you do not have to follow through with the second or third questions.

The parent must remember not to get upset because of a bad choice on the child's part. The more reactive we are, the more it shows that we are taking on their responsibility and ultimately, we will try to control the child. Then, on days when that child is mad at us and would like to watch us bounce off the walls, he simply pulls out of his repertoire some behavior he knows will drive us absolutely crazy. Be careful, then, not to let them see you sweat.

Be sure you have clear boundaries of responsibility with your children so that the consequences of their choices are *their* problems, which you can allow. Do not become angry at or fearful about them when they experience reasonably unpleasant consequences.

Make certain you are comfortable with your children making choices. God is comfortable with letting us make choices, even though the stakes are high. God also does not take His love to the far corner of heaven when we make a bad choice. He does not withdraw His support or understanding when we have sunk to our necks in our humanity, carnality, self-absorption, etc.); there's nothing wrong with being human! He wants us, and our kids, to develop an inner radar that will stand the test of time and circumstances; self-control from the inside out. Nurturing and developing genuine self-control from the inside out—the only place from which it can come, is a critical component of effective parenting.

How to Keep an Attitude

Webster's defines attitude as "a mental position or feeling with regard to a fact or state." Beliefs fuel values, values fuel attitudes, and attitudes fuel actions.

How many times have we seen or heard of young people going off to college or leaving their home, only to drastically change their beliefs about God, life, and what is important? Have you ever wondered why some youth retain the beliefs nurtured in their families and others seem quick to reject them?

As homeschooling parents, we clearly are invested in pointing our children to certain ways of thinking and toward particular views of the world. If we are pouring ourselves into our children, how can we be sure they will retain the important beliefs and attitudes about life as they make their way into adulthood?

Research in attitude inoculation can shed light on this subject. Attitude inoculation consists of measures to strengthen valued opinions or beliefs and to minimize the vulnerability to competing views. For many of us in homeschooling, we are careful to protect our children from too much of the pressures and brutalities of the world. We don't want them hurt by its hardness nor do we want them to adopt its ways. But research suggests that carefully exposing our children to values that compete with the ones we promote will be the best way to produce permanence in their beliefs.

Just as certain medical conditions and diseases can be prevented by being inoculated with a small amount of the neutralized disease, so too can beliefs be inoculated by exposing people to the counter arguments in a neutralized form. This neutralized form amounts to the argument against the argument, that is, why the opposing view is incorrect. The idea here is that some exposure to the other views, in a controlled setting where parents can help the child think through these issues, makes for a well-entrenched belief.

However, failure by parents to help children understand the prevailing arguments against their beliefs leads to a naive adherence. Like a plant raised indoors, when it is set out in the summer sun without a "hardening" process, it can die. With sudden exposure in college or other life situations to the counter arguments, young people are often so caught off guard that they lose trust in what they know.

Parents who are afraid of their children losing their faith or taking on odd beliefs are tempted to keep all mention of "the other side" away from their children so they won't be seduced into that thinking. Unfortunately, a complete absence of the other side leaves the child with no guiding or corrective thoughts. If given these reasons ahead of time, the child can replay the logic he learned when his beliefs are challenged. In short, too much protection is an avoidance which leaves the child most vulnerable in later years.

A few examples follow. When discussing certain doctrines of the Christian faith, I like to let children know what Muslim, Jewish, and the Far Eastern faiths such as Hinduism and Buddhism think regarding that particular doctrine. Letting the child know how others would disagree or perhaps even criticize our position is helpful as they gain some understanding of the big picture. We don't have to be negative or flippant about the other perspectives, but we can give a clear message to the child about where we stand and why we think ours is the most logical position.

Similarly, we can expose children to competing social or political positions in order to build and firm up the reasoning that backs your position. Of course, children are free to think and even disagree with us. We must be big enough psychologically to let them think without undue pressure. More and more they will adopt some ways of thinking and living life that are personalized to them and not just the way they were taught at home. This is the way of life. However, if we have not explained why we believe a doctrine or value, then we have not explored the reason why counter arguments are not compelling, and we have let them down making them more vulnerable than we imagined.

Dr. Dale Simpson

The next time you are having a good conversation about faith or other important beliefs, don't back off from a few words of education about the other side. Remember the research. Remember how we are inoculated against measles. Your children will have a better time holding on to what is true as they leave your direct influence in the years to come.

Chapter 1 Application

1. How does giving your children choices strengthen them? Does it seem permissive? Why?

2. Are you a self-controlled person in stressful times? What areas are harder or easier for you to be self-controlled in? Do you see any similar patterns in your children?

3. How did your parents control themselves under stress?

4. Do you see over-compliance in your parents, yourself, or your children? Can this be dangerous? Why?

5. Do you consciously teach your child to be a strong decision maker? Are you trying to control your child or teach him self-control?

6. Do you tend to hover over your child, bark orders at him, or consult with him, as he decides?

7. If you argue with your children, review the Three Question Method instead. Use this method with your children this week.

Chapter 2: Boundaries

Thou shalt not steal.

-Exodus 20:15

A chore chart hangs on our refrigerator door. It clearly states who empties the dishwasher on Tuesdays, who cleans the kitchen after dinner on Wednesdays, and so on. Without this chart, daily responsibilities would not be accomplished without many problems. The chart clearly states who is responsible for what chore. That makes the house run smoothly. These lines of responsibility also exist in interpersonal relationships. Teaching your child to be responsible for emotions, thoughts, and behaviors will determine how healthy his or her relationships will be throughout life.

Besides becoming strong decision makers, our children must learn what is theirs to decide and to control. They must know the boundaries where they can invest their energy and capabilities. Boundaries have to do with identity, personal responsibility and the sense of self. The awareness of self is not selfishness, but rather something God has built into us that emerges during the course of life. It is something necessary for directing one's life effectively. "Self" is not the problem. We are always selves—just false or true selves, loving or fearful selves, mature or immature selves, etc.

Somewhere in the formative years, the realization sets in that you are responsible for yourself. You did not ask to be born. You did not ask to be created. It was not your choice. But now that you're here, you are responsible for your life.

Children need to understand this. They must develop a sense of responsibility for what happens within their boundaries. This is a learned process. Who you are, what you are responsible for and what you need to address in your life is not something inherent. When does this differentiation of a sense of self begin? It begins during the terrible two's (eighteen to thirty-six months of age), when children learn that by saying "no," they can make the giants bounce off the walls.

Do you know how intoxicating it is for a little person to say, "No!" and have two big people not know what to do? The little one loves it. It's their first awareness of a part of them that isn't Mom or Dad. It's "me," not "you."

This growing awareness crops up all through the formative years, especially during the teenage years when they become intoxicated all over again. During this time, they want to be sure they know who is "me" and not "you." They want to feel older and not like a child influenced by a parent.

The intellectually sharp or strong-willed kids will often push harder than others. They will test every rule or position you have. I believe they are used by God to make us face our own standards and choices. We need to be sure our values are well thought out and biblical rather than just our control issues masquerading as biblical. How parents handle a child's growing self-awareness is critical.

Boundaries must be experienced in relation to other people. As stated earlier, healthy living requires us to have a clear sense of who we are and what we are responsible for. Those of you who had parents with a good sense of responsibility and a good sense of boundaries have a pretty good sense of boundaries, too. It's going to be easier for you to know how to react to your children's testing.

It's going to be easier for you to know how to answer the question, "Whose problem is this?" when a kid knocks a baseball through a neighbor's window. You will know whose problem it is. Those of you who grew up in living situations where people did not have clear boundaries will have a problem with this.

What does it mean not to have good boundaries? Parents who get repeatedly upset and are reactive to a child's bad choices have poor boundaries. Parents who use shame, guilt, and manipulation to control children have poor boundaries. That is not to say all guilty feelings are bad. There are healthy and unhealthy guilt feelings. However, when you are forcing someone to act right by using feelings of guilt, you're the one attempting to control. You're the one with a poor sense of boundaries.

Parents who are crushed over a child's unhappiness have poor boundaries. If your child has experienced a disappointment and you can't sleep at night because of their frustration, you have a poor sense of boundaries. Parents who react to a child's poor choice as though it was a personal attack on them have poor boundaries. Parents who rescue and enable children by over-helping and minimizing reasonable consequences have poor boundaries.

The Book of Proverbs talks about wise choices and self-control. It discusses controlling your temper, your greed, your mouth, your lust, your sexual appetites - everything. It also says, "Do not rescue a man prone to a bad temper for if you do, you will only have to do it again." (Prov.19:19) Isn't that challenging? I don't think it would be stretching Scripture to say that you should not rescue people from any reasonable consequences stemming from their own misbehavior. We should be nurturing, but not rescuing from proper consequences.

Have you ever known somebody who keeps "rescuing" their child and then is befuddled as to why, year after year, the child keeps getting into more trouble and ends up with a criminal record? The parents don't see their role in this scenario. Their own sense of pain, guilt, and fear for the child gets so blurred, the parents start doing things they have no business doing. If you try to rescue your children and shield them so much that you prevent them from going through a reasonable frustration in life, you have unclear boundaries with your children.

Do not rescue people from reasonable consequences. Does that mean to let people drown? Of course not. Don't let people starve. Don't let them drown. But don't always sweep up the crumbs in their life or you'll have someone who can't make tough choices in this world. They'll be waiting for you to make the choices for them. They'll be waiting for the probation officer to make the choices or for somebody else to manage their life. They'll wait in vain for someone to make the bad consequences go away. They will think that anyone who doesn't eliminate their pain is unloving.

Good boundaries will find us encouraging choice in our children. Allowing, initiating, and supporting reasonable consequences for misbehavior will be standard procedure. Accept your children's feelings and little idiosyncrasies. They can feel something you don't feel and that's okay. You may not understand it, you may not agree with it, and you may not think it is spiritually or emotionally mature (and it may not be!). But if they're feeling it, please be big enough to show some sense of acknowledgment and acceptance of those feelings before you do anything else.

Your children are different from you. They're not supposed to be clones. Too often we try to control because we don't like what they're feeling; we don't like what they're thinking. We start behaving on automatic pilot. We say things that, if recorded, would embarrass us.

Have you ever caught yourself doing that? I have. I'll stop and think, "I hope I'm not on Candid Camera." I hope nobody has a video somewhere. I wouldn't want anyone to see that I'm really not tuned into what is going on with the child — I'm really doing something to make me feel better. I'm doing something to reassure myself that they're not going to do this again because of my lecture."

There's a place for talking, don't get me wrong. But you need to accept what they're feeling, even if it's unpleasant feelings toward you. Remember, there's acceptance and then there's non-disciplining. These are two different concepts. Be sure you can accept when they are angry with you. Teach them how to handle anger properly. When they're frightened and you don't think they ought to be, help them understand that sometimes you get scared too, that some things in life are scary.

Good boundaries find us acting as consultants rather than dictators or over-involved busybodies. We can err in three extremes: neglect, barking orders, or protecting them so much we make too many decisions for them. We can teach too many lessons too many times instead of letting the consequences speak to them.

If we have good boundaries, we treat ourselves with respect and we'll expect our children to treat us with respect. Parents who allow their children to yell and scream at them disrespectfully wonder why the kids continue to do it. It's because the children pay attention, they're alert, and they see it's okay with you. Parents who get caught in this situation often end up nagging, asking, bargaining, or begging the child over and over not to talk like that but nothing changes.

Nagging doesn't enable the child to be a strong decision maker (in a situation) because they don't know where the boundaries are in relation to showing respect. What happens when they grow up, get a job and start behaving that way? Others don't put up with it out there in the world. What happens if they talk like that to some guy on the street who pulls out a knife? The guy may not care about them the way Mama did. It will be too late to learn the lesson.

Good boundaries find us refusing to be our children's consciences, but rather letting their consciences develop. The more you nag, the less reason they have to use their conscience. They'll be waiting for you to tell them even if it's the eighth, ninth, tenth time.

Kids learn where your action threshold is. Is ten times your threshold? If so, they learn that the tenth time is when you lose your temper. You think it's the anger that made them respond, but they know it's the tenth time and you're ready to act. If you whispered instead of yelled and they knew every time you whispered you were getting ready to act, they would respond when you whispered. It's not the anger, I assure you. It's when you finally get to the point of doing something about it.

Try whispering sometime. They won't know what you're doing! "Honey, I have something important to tell you. If you do not turn off the Nintendo right now, I'll have to do something you will not like," says Luke's father. Luke responds, "Like what?" "I don't know dear, but I promise, you will not like it." "Why would you do that?" asks Luke. "Because I love you," answers Luke's father.

When somebody is going to do something because they love you, they are really committed to it. You can't talk them out of it. The only thing worse they could hear is, "God told me to." They know they're not going to talk you out of that one.

I like to look in their cute little eyes and say, "Honey, I love you and you have a choice. You can either do it or not do it. It's really up to you. But if you won't do it, here's what I am going to do. If you will do it, I'll be a happy camper and we'll be in great shape." Some of you are afraid to let your kids have these choices. But what you don't realize is that they make the choices anyway. You're just not paying attention. Sometimes you bark out an order and they do it. You think your order made them obey. No, they made a choice to do it.

Choice or Consequence

As we stated earlier, when children have the responsibility to make choices, they need to know over what domain they have control. What kind of template can we use to decide what the parent is responsible for and what the child is responsible for?

I have four criteria I use as a convenient template for me when I'm trying to answer the crucial question, "Whose problem is this?" Let's examine our responsibilities.

1. Thoughts
Our thoughts and beliefs are in our control. Ultimately what children think and believe is in their domain. We try sometimes to persuade and educate but the ultimate power to think about and believe something is theirs.

2. Feelings
Their feelings, as we said earlier, are their own. If they're truly feeling something, it's silly to tell them they're not or that they shouldn't. Telling them they shouldn't minimizes their life, and it doesn't stop the feeling, it just makes them go underground with the feeling when around you. Feelings are neither right nor wrong. They simply are—and that goes for any age, by the way.

3. Actions

We have different responses based on what we've learned to do with feelings. For example, two people get angry. One responds by throwing a frying pan and the other by saying, "I'm really angry about what you did." Two different responses. The reactions are based on what we have learned to do with anger. We are in charge of our behavior no matter what anyone else does to us.

4. Happiness
When I say happiness, I mean peace of mind regardless of the circumstances. Those of us who have seen it in the Bible call it "Joy." Whatever you call it, it's an overall peace of mind regardless of the circumstances. It's not just having a fleeting thrill. You can have lots of thrills and be miserable. You probably won't be miserable during the thrill but you may after the thrill dies away. If thrills equaled happiness, then crack addicts should be the happiest people on the planet. Instead, they are among the most miserable people because they keep searching for the thrill they just lost. Happiness is a by-product of godly and healthy choices.

These four criteria are the template to determine our circle of responsibility. If it has to do with MY thoughts, MY feelings, MY actions or MY peace of mind (happiness), then it's MY problem. If it has to do with my child's thoughts, feelings, actions or happiness, then it sounds like it's their problem. Of course, when we make someone important to us, they influence and impact us. We are not islands without the capacity to be moved or affected. But clear responsibilities and boundaries make good relationships.

As a parent I have a serious responsibility. I have to help my children come to terms with their problem. It's my job to structure the environment, and structure my interaction with them so they can grow into accepting responsibility for their life and managing it effectively.

Chapter 2 Application

1. Think about your family of origin. Was there a clear respect for your individuality? Were personal boundaries respected? Were you allowed the space for your own thoughts and feelings?

2. When your child expresses thoughts or feelings different from your own, how do you respond?

3. Do you knock before you open doors? What are other examples of family boundaries besides doors?

4. Who do you think is responsible for your child's happiness? Do you feel guilty when your child is unhappy? If yes, what do you do to resolve your guilt?

5. Can you allow your children to suffer consequences without carrying their pain? Can you allow consequences to teach without adding punishment?

Dr. Dale Simpson

Chapter 3: Legacies to Leave Your Children

Virtue and genuine graces in themselves speak what no words can utter.

-William Shakespeare

Have you ever thought about your tombstone? What message would you like your family to inscribe on that tombstone? The life you live today will determine the inscription you leave on your children's lives.

Each of us will leave some kind of legacy — some history, some tradition, something left behind that will profoundly affect the lives of our family members. What legacies do you want to leave your children?

Are you living your life in a way that will help you achieve your goals? Think about what you want to leave your children, and what you have to do to ensure these values are built into the system. We have the control to make the story come out the way we want if we deal with things today.

What teachings will you leave your family? Someone once said there are two educations: one teaches us how to make a living, and the other how to live. The greatest legacy you can leave is having taught your children a way to live. A fellow once said, "What a father says to his children is not heard by the world, but it will be heard by posterity." It will be heard in the next generation. In a negative way, all the shouting, all the threats, all the things nobody else hears is internalized by our children. Then they grow up and act it out, and then, too late, we see who we were. This is a legacy some have mistakenly chosen. Thankfully, we can contemplate and plan our legacies now, before it's too late.

The number one legacy I want to leave my children is a legacy of godliness. Those of us who look at things from a theological perspective know that in many ways we are like God to our children. We define reality to them, guiding and influencing them. It's an awesome responsibility. If we come from a Judeo-Christian background, we also call God our Father. They will see the unseen God through the visible parents and will interpret the world through them. They will learn if relationships are safe, if it's safe to relate to God, if it's safe to relate to other people.

It is critical when teaching godliness to be careful to relate to the emotional needs of the child. For example, a five- year-old in Sunday school needs to feel loved, accepted, and to feel worthwhile. Don't teach complex theological concepts to a five-year-old. Don't think teaching godliness is primarily an intellectual or cognitive activity. Teach them to feel good about being in God's house with God's people. If they get that, then they might be open to other things as they cognitively and intellectually mature. They need to feel affirmed so that when they're told how much God loves them, they have something to compare it to.

Of course, trying to pass on godliness to our children means that first and foremost we have to live it. We must integrate it into our daily lives. Deuteronomy 11:19 says of God's ways, "Teach them to your children, talking about them when you sit at home and when you walk along the road, when you lie down and when you get up." You show God and interpret God to your children throughout the whole day. It doesn't have to feel spiritual to be spiritual, and some things that feel spiritual aren't. Using religious words without genuineness undercuts true religious teaching. As a parent, personal godliness must be sought if we want to produce godliness in our children.

Leave a legacy that is based on more than just telling them the "don'ts." There are plenty of "don'ts" in this world and it's okay to share them with the child, but we have to leave more. We must live, not just talk, family values. We must show self-control and set limits for ourselves. Firm limits show our children the self-control that reflects godliness. We must also show affirming things in life.

The second legacy would be to instill in our children the ability to love and be loved. Children are generally reflectors of love instead of generators of it. Inside, in some form or another, they're always asking, "Am I loved?" It's a built-in thing. We all have an intrinsic need to be accepted and loved by somebody in this world. Frankly, there are over five billion people in the world who do not care whether you and I live or die. We don't need to please everybody or to have everybody love us and think we're great, but to have at least one significant person securely love us. Once we realize that if one person can love us, another person might do it, then we can face life with some peace.

Love begins with love. Children internalize our ability to love first. They take it in, they internalize it, they identify with us and take our behavior as a statement about their lovability. Whatever they receive from us, they act on and believe. If we want them to know how to love well, we must know how to give love.

People who had loving parents come into parenting with more resources than those who didn't. Some of you come from an environment of inconsistency, maybe alcoholism, drug addiction, something in the parents that made them really off center in some areas. You did not get consistent, reliable love, and you never learned to internalize it. That's probably why some are pleasers or why some can't develop close relationships. Some people try to avoid relationships altogether. Many men just don't know how to get close. They never felt truly accepted by anybody so they have a deep-rooted fear of being so unlovable. They believe that if you get to know them too well you would be scared away. If you get a little close to some people, they back off or do something to sabotage the relationship. You thought being close was supposed to make you feel closer. It makes some people feel afraid. It's often their attempt to control the fear of not being loved.

We must be a vessel of love to our children and show them they are truly safe with us even when they mess up. We're like the containment vessel around a nuclear reactor that has walls of reinforced concrete. It's considered safe to turn the reactor on because if a little puff of radioactive steam comes out, it's okay. We have a structure to contain it. If we don't have containment, we're afraid to turn it on, and if a mistake were to happen, we're in bigger trouble.

This is how it is with life. Children are going to make mistakes, and they need to know our love is the containment vessel; it is rock solid. Even when they mess up, even when they don't like us and are angry, even when they disobey us, the love and acceptance part is not going to go away.

When the love and acceptance isn't consistent, it's often called "conditional love." If the love and connectedness leaves when a child messes up, and comes back when they're good, the child can become insecure.

They try to figure ways to control your love by being good or making good grades. There isn't anything wrong with being good or making good grades, but if a child thinks they control love in that manner, they'll probably become perfectionists when they're older because they fear failure.

They haven't learned to relax with their humanity in a relationship.

The solution isn't anything radical. We, as parents, must teach our children the ability to love and be loved. We can't give away what we don't have; therefore, we must feed daily on God's holy and constant love for us. People who know how to feel love can then give it to their spouse, their children, their friends, their fellow church members. They'll know how to give it because they aren't preoccupied with receiving it.

We want to be sure we can love in a self-controlled way. Be the containment vessel for your children. Set clear limits for them and allow them to make mistakes, then let them know they're still safe with us. Discipline with nurturance and connectedness.

We have to be sure we're good enough love-givers to get back in the relational game when mistakes happen. It's tough when kids do something wrong and you feel you don't like them for it. It's easy to avoid them emotionally and when they feel the displeasure in your voice, they know what's happening. They feel the love suddenly go away, and they're estranged.

How does this make the child feel? Scared. And they'll try to do something to make the love come back. Some children, after feeling chronically defeated, give up on obtaining the love. Then, in their despair, they settle for material things and pleasure instead of relationships.

We want them to know our love for them is secure no matter what happens. "You know if you end up in jail, Honey, I'll be there during visiting hours and I'll pray for you. There isn't anything you could do to make me stop loving you. Nobody can keep my heart from loving you." In 400 B.C. Euripides said, "He is not a lover who does not love forever."

Jesus said, "Greater love hath no man than this, that he would lay down his life for his friends." We wouldn't hesitate to throw ourselves in front of a speeding car for our family, or take a bullet for them if somebody were shooting at us. But there are other ways to give up your life. Like biting your tongue when it would feel so good to say something. That's dying to yourself. Are you going to give up your life to help them come to terms with things or are you going to get angry at them and pout, distancing yourself from your child? Are you going to punish them with your silence?

It's devastating to a child when you are not engaged with them fully, i.e. physically, emotionally, mentally and spiritually. To me, giving up my life for my family is probably not going to be jumping in front of a speeding car. It's going to be something harder. It's going to be the daily sacrificial choosing of love over selfishness.

The third legacy I hope to leave to my children is how to work with a godly attitude. Isn't this something your children will need in their lives? I talked to a lady recently who told me her children never had to do any chores. Sounds like a great place to live, except they're learning something wrong. They're learning that it's somebody else's job to maintain their lives. Somebody once said, "Millions of Americans are not working, but thank the Lord they've got jobs."

In order to teach the concept of working with a good attitude, we need to work alongside our children. The younger they are, the more we need to be there with them. When you're helping a five-year-old clean up her room, you sit down on the floor with her and say, "Honey, I'll get the toys over here, and you get the ones over there and we'll clean it up together." Or, when you have big mounds of clothes to fold, the five-year-old can help pull out the socks. That's all, no big thing. This is how you teach them to work. You do it with them and talk about things while you're doing it. This is a wonderful place to start. Just be sure your children have reasonable chores that are age appropriate.

Unfortunately, I've known some families who use their children as little slaves. The parents are busy so the kids have to do everything. They hate doing an hour and a half of work every day. I would too if I were thirteen or fourteen years old. So be sensitive, work with them, and help them associate work with positive things that are happening. Be playful while you work. Kids need to play a lot. That's their job — to be a kid and learn how to live life. We need to integrate regular chores and regular activities as just a part of life.

One last cautionary note - we need to be careful of the danger of falling into workaholism. We want to teach our kids that work is important, but we need to have a balance. That's a proper, godly view of work. God wants us to do a good job but not hold up perfection or excellence to the point that it gets out of balance. Because, number one, perfection is not attainable, and number two, an excellent life is a balanced life.

Chapter 3 Application

1. What characteristics did you get from your parents? Which ones do you like? Which ones do you dislike? Did they teach you through words or actions?

2. With words, what do you teach your child? Do you exhibit these concepts with your actions? With actions, what do you teach?

3. What are you pleased to see in your child? How can you build on that?

4. Many positive traits are not revealed until your child is a young adult. Which traits do you think will show up later in your child's life?

5. How would you rate yourself in your ability to give love? In your ability to be firm? How would you rate your mate's ability to give love? In your mate's ability to be firm?

6. In your child's life, who are the people who have the ability to love well?

7. Family Activity - Look at pictures of your parents and in-laws and discuss them with your child. Tell your child stories about their grandparents or great-grandparents.

Dr. Dale Simpson

Chapter 4: Successfully Navigating the Digital Life

"My Internet went down for five minutes, so I went downstairs and spoke with my family. They seem like nice people."

Douglas Gresham, CS Lewis' stepson, said, "In today's world, we look at our presidents, our prime ministers, our princes and our potentates and we look to them as our leaders, but they are not. They are merely our rulers. The leaders are the people who change the minds and stimulate the imaginations of the public, whether of children or adults. That means the moviemakers, the people who make TV shows, the entertainment people in the business." (And might we update his list to include social media moguls, internet moguls, and software designers.)

She was 17 years old with learning problems, social awkwardness, and a canyon full of self-doubt. The needy girl made her way to the city airport and waited excitedly for Andy, with whom she would spend the weekend. Never had she felt this attractive and desirable, light years away from the low self-esteem she always carried with her. This would be the most amazing weekend ever and she fully expected to be treated like a queen.

She met Andy on a Christian teen chat site, sharing hours of messages and emails over many weeks. Well into their online relationship, and after she was starting to have feelings for him, he shared that he was not really a teenager but an adult who thought she was the greatest person ever. He could not wait to spend time with her and to do anything that would make her happy. The girl was so taken by the person behind the emails that any caution she might have had vanished long ago. He was so nice and he made her feel special. Her empty bucket of self-esteem was now filled with a newfound value never before experienced. She felt weightless and nothing else mattered.

Moments before the visitor landed, her frantic parents found her. They had discovered the emails which led them to the airport, frightened that they might not get there in time, wondering if they would ever see their daughter again. They could imagine the weekend plans a 42-year-old, recently released ex-convict, had for their child.

This true story ended well, but many online connections do not.

The internet. A metaphorical neighborhood where every kind of person lives. Residents will try to contact you for a variety of reasons, not the least of which is to get clicks and also money. It's also a neighborhood where pedophiles hide behind trees. Many good families live in this area too. However, in a few houses there are people who run sex trafficking rings. In a few other houses there are corporations who don't care at all about you, but who only want more money and power. How will you navigate this neighborhood with so many benefits and so many dangers?

The world is not the same as it was decades ago, or even just a few years ago. Because of the rapid expansion of technology, our modern times are unlike the time our ancestors experienced. "Change is the process by which the future invades our lives," as one author put it "shifting our values and shriveling our roots."

Alvin Toffler, in his 1970 book, Future Shock, confronted us with the challenging reality that change is not only happening, but it is happening at a rapidly increasing rate. Children back then (and even more so today) grew up in a much different world than their parents. An eight-year-old child is not living the same life that his or her parent lived at that age. Now, each generation experiences such a different world during their formative years that the way children think and feel about life is often completely alien to their parents. We have moved from hunter-gatherers to domestic agriculturalists to the industrial age, and now to the age of information – the digital age – challenging us like nothing else before it.

Advancements in technology and human capability are speeding along at an ever-increasing rate, and we are unable to see what the future effects (or side effects) will be on developing children as well as the human species. If and when we find that a technology is "bad for us," it will be too late. Even now, researchers are exploring the effects of technology on the central nervous system and brain development of young children who are heavy consumers of "screens." We do not know yet whether these changes will help or hinder life in the future. Toffler wondered whether human beings could psychologically handle being bombarded by so much information, and by change itself. We are left unable to control the rate and degree of change. We can only trail further and further behind the rapidity of change, measuring things after the fact rather than directing or controlling change.

Toffler, looking at the future in 1970, got many things right, including the transience of our relationships with each other and with things; that a virtual reality would be as comfortable as reality itself; the emergence of powerful cyborgs and artificial intelligence; the overstimulation of children; and the prominence of super-empowered individuals (instant billionaires, anyone?).

Watch old black-and-white films, or even films from the '60s and '70s. See how slowly people walk across a room, how long the scenes are compared to films today. These movies have a different presentation of time. It's all in slow motion to us now. The advent of Sesame Street and its rapid-fire multisensory methods was a major turning point in changing young children's brain development. The acceleration of change is seriously affecting each of us in untold ways. Parents of young children were themselves kids raised on digital and fast-paced stimuli, and their kids even more so. Young parents already have a digi-life.

In a secular world, teens and adults alike look for security in technology and the rapid expanse of knowledge, innovations, and solutions. Yet many don't find security. Many teens and young adults don't want to grow up. Facing so many choices can be overwhelming for kids, and maybe for adults, too. Video choices, music choices, social media connections—there are a seemingly unending number of choices and demands for frenetic lifestyles, all under the bombardment of advertising.

Dr. Kathy Koch, director of Creative Kids, says teens today are "tech addicted, tired, stressed, overwhelmed, depressed, and escaping." Even many teenagers will admit they are afraid of being addicted to their devices. On ABC's "Good Morning America," as 12 and 13-year-olds discussed their life with screens, one youngster said, "I've had one of those nights where [I was] like, 'I need my phone!' So, I constructed this myself. It's my fake phone." He needed the comfort of a fake phone, like a teddy bear, or a technological security blanket.

Let's face it. It is impossible for you as a parent to keep track of the interactions your children have through digital means. The irony is, these large companies (not only social media companies) know more about your child in some areas as they pass through the formative years than you do. Because of greed, corporations and people in power are likely more motivated and more skilled at data mining than even the intelligence departments of the world's nations. Even as I write this, Google and Facebook are under serious scrutiny as we learn how much information they collect on average citizens like you and me, using it to direct our behavior and make money.

Four- and five-year-old kids know exactly what Facebook, Twitter, and other social media are. They see teens and adults using them all the time. Even though they don't have an account, they sense that these are things people do and that this is normal life. They want to participate in what teenagers and grown-ups like to do.

On average, text messages are read in under 5 seconds (SlickText, a text marketing company). It takes 90 seconds for the typical receiver to respond to a text (CTIA, the trade organization for the wireless industry). Young adults 18 – 24 years old send and receive over 128 text every day (Experian Marketing Services). Our lives are continually interrupted by beeps and bops, technological cues that have conditioned us, even our kids. Like Pavlov's dogs, we are conditioned in a world that's become a laboratory. People outside our families, people we do not know and with whom we may not share similar values, decide what is popular, how we will behave, and what things we will purchase. Understanding the effects of power, wealth, manipulation, conditioning, and greed on our society is not the subject for this book. But the average citizen has no idea how much money and research are dedicated in order to shape his or her everyday life. And consistent manipulation works. It would shock you to realize how much your choices are determined by others.

Just imagine what the algorithm looks like that allows you to type in a few words or partial words. Then in .6 seconds the search engine produces pages of results, sometimes ten thousand pages. And now, the user is looking at the most expensive piece of real estate in the world: the first page of a Google search. Companies pay to be listed at the top of this first page when certain words or combinations of words are searched. What you are looking at is a completely manipulated landscape designed to keep your attention and deliver your money to others. Have you ever scrolled down more than three or four pages, much less 100 or 1000? As we look at the first page, we are now under their spell and they are throwing every psychological and marketing trick at us as fast as they can. Their onslaught will follow you wherever you go online. Cookies and other information are taken from your computer and from your online activity to continuously refine what companies know about you. They take this digital information, and in milliseconds present personalized ads on your screen because they use other powerful algorithms and formulas to predict how you think, what you want, and how you feel.

Sean Parker, the first president of Facebook, talks about the behavioral conditioning that he and others cleverly and purposefully built into your interaction with Facebook: "We need to sort of give you a little dopamine hit every once in a while, because someone liked or commented on a photo or a post or whatever… And that's going to get you to contribute more content, and that's going to get you…more likes and comments." He continues, "You want people using your product because it's a part of [their] life, then they can't stop using it." And along with this, Facebook has all the elements of high school drama on steroids. Remember, Facebook was created on a school campus.

Parker said that he and Facebook CEO and co-founder Mark Zuckerberg (among other social media entrepreneurs) understood that they were launching a website that could be addicting. Not surprisingly, he says, "We did it anyway." He continues, "The thought process that went into building these applications, Facebook being the first of them…was all about: 'How do we consume as much of your time and conscious attention as possible?'" As a result, billions of unnecessary interruptions happen every day. Welcome to social media.

Speaking of Facebook, Parker added that it "literally changes your relationship with society, with each other." He also went on to call the social media giant "a social-validation feedback loop" that exploits a core vulnerability in the human psyche. "God only knows what it's doing to our children's brains," he said.

They use our social nature to manipulate us. For instance, it is rude not to answer someone's email. Similarly, Facebook and LinkedIn ask you to do one simple thing such as endorse someone you know. Then they show other people you possibly know and ask you to connect to them. Sometimes it implies that they are connecting you with others and want you to reciprocate. And all you wanted to do was endorse your friend as a good worker.

Loren Brichter, the designer who created the slot-machine-like pull-down-to-refresh mechanism now widely used on smartphones, confessed: "Pull-to-refresh is addictive. Twitter is addictive. These are not good things. When I was working on them, it was not something I was mature enough to think about. I'm not saying I'm mature now, but I'm a little bit more mature, and I regret the downsides."

And Roger McNamee, an investor in Facebook and Google, said the strategies of people who run Facebook and Google "have led to horrific unintended consequences… The problem is that there is nothing the companies can do to address the harm unless they abandon their current advertising (manipulation) models." And that, of course, they will not do. His comments are part of a wave of tech figures expressing disillusionment and concern about the products they helped build.

Tristan Harris points out how we are manipulated: controlling the menu controls our choices, making us fear that we are missing something (fear of missing something important: FOMSI). This plays on people's need for social approval, bombards us with infinite feeds, sets autoplay to "on," and provides constant interruptions. Like an inconsiderate person, our devices routinely "break in line," getting ahead of us and our activities, having no concern for us.

Here is a partial list of the potential hazards of living in a digital world.

1. Target #1. You are the target for every psychological and conditioning strategy that every business, politician, and government uses to control both societal and individual behavior. You are the conditioned one and they are the conditioners. You are one of Pavlov's drooling dogs, a trained rat in a Skinner Box.

Powerful scientific methods have long since left the laboratory and entered into each family's life. Variable interval reinforcement is one technique that maximizes the conditioning; that is to say, it makes the person or animal persist in the target behavior.

Psychologists figured this truth out years ago, applying its power in many settings, including the casino. From slot machines to card games, you play a losing game against the house. The "deep" variable reinforcement schedule creates irrational, addictive behavior which binds the person to their chair. Like a symbiotic host on another animal, they want to suck most of the life out without killing the host. They want you back so they can continue to get rich while you suffer.

Networks can manufacture trends, manipulate ways of thinking, and flood channels by impersonating real people. As AI develops, we will see this manipulation even more. Governments can shape foreign elections for far less than the cost of a fighter plane.

2. The Feeding of Impulsivity. The teenage desire for acceptance and popularity is now fueled by a constant demand to respond quickly, to keep up, and to be relevant. Our children are able to communicate 24 hours a day, and often without parental scrutiny. Posting pictures, updating, and texting all demand that kids react. We know their prefrontal lobes are responsible for self-control and judgment, and yet they are not well developed in childhood or adolescence. This leaves them vulnerable to impulsiveness without considering future consequences. An uncertain, fragile sense of self and identity sets them up for exploitation.

A child's world is often filled with quips like, "I got so many likes this week," or "Look at how many people are following me," or "One hundred people retweeted my tweet." So many kids are desperate to fit in and to feel okay about themselves (a normal need), and yet it can sound like young people are shouting out to others, "Look! Somebody likes me!" We all want to be liked, especially middle schoolers and teenagers, but what used to be a milder process is now more intense and overtly acted out in everyday life. Instant information. Instant popularity. Instant gratification for our need to be connected, liked, noticed, and admired. But the power of it can also lead to instant social death.

3. The Lack of Privacy. Like Las Vegas, "What goes happens on the internet, stays on the internet." And yet phone messages go to other phones. Phone images go to other phones. And we know young people frequently do not think about the consequences of their actions. Kids still think others can keep a secret. They can't. When certain things are splattered on the internet and therefore throughout the school, it can be devastating to a young person who is unsure of him or herself and desperate to fit in.

4. Immediate Gratification. Kathy Koch points out that our world is the "now," with people growing more and more impatient. The experience and addictive nature of immediate feedback shapes our behavior. Our screens and those apps we are using communicate back to us quickly, causing us to continue our gaze. For additional money you can bypass the lines at Disney World or Universal Studios with a special pass. Soon, it will only take one day to receive the item that you ordered online, and eventually, purchases will be delivered in a few hours (that is, if you don't create the item at home with 3D printing!). From buildings to food items, there will be less and less time between what you can imagine or desire and its fulfillment. Waiting is passé. Instant is the new norm. Waiting is for losers.

5. The Culture of New. Koch argues that we live in "a culture of new." The very new equals "good," and the recently old equals "bad." Even as I write this, I know that much of what I'm saying will be outdated if you are reading this a few years after it is published. Does buying a five-year-old computer or game system

sound enticing? Maybe our time in history should be called the "now, new, never-ending, never satisfying, never stopping world."

6. Failure to Launch. We are witnessing an increased number of young people who don't want to grow up. They are not interested in getting their driver's license as soon as they are eligible. They don't want to face what's out there, with many feeling extremely anxious and fearful that they don't have the competencies to be successful.

What causes this? Maybe the sedentary life doesn't need anything "out there." Everything one needs is in the house or apartment: food, Wi-Fi, a digital social life, social media, and games. Is this what Toffler feared when he warned that people in the rapidly changing future might be "doomed to a massive adaptational breakdown." Is this the adaptational breakdown we are witnessing today? Research continues to show that the more media kids use, the less empathic they are, findings that follow them right into college.

7. Bullying Magnified. A 12-year-old girl, after continuous bullying on social media by two other girls (at a school having "zero tolerance" for bullying), committed suicide after feeling hopelessly battered and worthless. The power of cyber-bullying crushed her sense of value and belonging, but in public for all to see. A young person can be intoxicated with online fame, and he or she can be so ashamed and embarrassed that they want to die, as some people have done when real or even false information has been posted to social media. Personal fame can occur throughout the world instantly online, even in a sad or negative way. Recently, another girl committed suicide online while live streaming the whole act and the lead up to it.

The internet is the new place where kids can impact others with no supervision and where children have no group support. Online dangerous dares have escalated such that young people video themselves engaging in illegal or potentially life-threatening activities in order to prove to their peer group they are not weak or afraid.

Cyber bullying is easier than bullying face-to-face. Our kids are bullied and threatened online. Most of them will be verbally abused online while playing socially interactive games. Kids can feel hopeless very quickly. The phrase "formative years" means exactly that: the time when young people develop, forming their core beliefs about themselves and the world.

8. The Stoking of Fear. Television media and particularly news programs manipulate us with two powerful emotions: fear and anger. From talk shows to coverage of terrorism, media moguls' priorities have nothing to do with giving you accurate information. Just like Facebook, their concern is only how long you watched a show, because it translates into money and influence for them. Anxiety and anger are the forces that bring you back.

Research tells us that heavy consumers of television and news programs think differently than those who consume less. This is a sign of the homogenization of experience and culture that began in earnest with home radios and really hit a stride when almost all families in the 1950s had a black-and-white television. Almost everyone saw the same shows, commercials, and news programs. Almost every home had a TV playing and dominating home life in the morning before work and from 6 p.m. to the time families went to bed. Families became addicted to television long before children and adults became addicted to their smart phones.

With radio and television, technology gave us the ability to experience things without leaving our homes. It also gave others who want our money a seat in our living room, a chair at our dining room table, and yes, even a voice in our conversations.

Corporations were there to manipulate and drive the mindset of our country following World War II. Consumerism promises a wonderful world where citizens continue to buy, industry continues to produce items to sell, everyone has a great job, and everyone should strive to have the things they don't have. The powerful have more than just a front row seat. They define what happens on stage. They write the play. We became the lab rats to train. Naïvely, we invited someone into our homes who would tell us how to think about ourselves (if you have dandruff, your coworkers will look down upon you) and how to solve our problems (buy their shampoo). They can provide answers to their own problems and show you how to be happy and contented (you need their product because it will make your life better and, thus, make you happy). They have a solution for the unhappiness they created. Buy more and more stuff. Buy newer stuff. Buy stuff you don't need. Show others your status by having more "toys" than they do. You must keep up with the Joneses. They have a new car. You must get a new car soon. The rats are learning their lessons well. Contentment and gratitude vanish under the onslaught of advertisements.

Facebook and Google make money only when they have your attention. Every second of your time (and your life) is a unit of income for them. They do not worry if you have more important things to do. They do not fret about your family, friends, or your individual well-being. Their anxieties are in the opposite direction. They worry about finding a new way to condition and shape your behavior. "Time spent" is the currency for which they compete. We are in an "Attention Economy," as media critic Tristan Harris described it. More than ever, time and attention equal money. Gaining and keeping your attention is the target, the bull's-eye, the winning score. And thousands of people are spending long hours and large budgets on controlling you. Without their staff and resources, overcoming these powerful influences in your life will take thoughtful effort.

"Fake news" is the popular phrase today, but all TV or newspaper news, and even written history, has been "manipulated news." Psychology knows that even if someone is not trying to distort, he or she can distort nonetheless. And some people are purposefully trying to show things their way, to manipulate their information, to make you think the way they wish. After The Battle of Kadesh, the great Pharaoh Ramesses II chiseled "news" of a victory over the Hittites when in fact it was, at best, a draw. Fortunately for the Pharaoh, the battle was far away, and most Egyptian citizens did not know the truth. And those who did know would have a very bad day if they were to reveal the truth. The Pharaoh declared victory and came home. His press agents started chiseling.

9. Tragedy Overload. Kathy Koch highlights a concern that many of us have. She makes the point that not many years ago, a tragedy was described mostly in print with an occasional picture sometimes hours after the event. Now it is instant, sometimes even live-streaming, and it is part of a visual and auditory onslaught. Many have chosen not to watch television news shows because of this onslaught and its accompanying manipulation, opting instead to get current events in a written form. What is the effect of repeated exposure to crises of all sorts: the tornadoes, the shootings, and the wars, with the repeated video of the carnage? Research unfolding in the last 20 years suggests it is not good.

10. Humans Need Limits. Even Sigmund Freud said this in his book Civilization and Its Discontents, arguing that without social rules and oversight, we would eventually kill each other. One limit and controlling factor, historically, has been that others knew much of what you were doing. Now, with modern transportation, a person can drive 100 miles to a destination and no one knows them. Much can be done on the internet with a fair amount of anonymity. The fewer negative consequences threatening humans, the less controlled they often become. The internal centrifugal force of curiosity and desire tends to push outward,

making hedonistic and antisocial behavior more likely in an anonymous world.

The internet super-highway can now take people across the globe. On the internet highway, people can be anonymous. The shy person communicates more than they would normally if face-to-face with someone. The angry, insecure kid can bully without the fear of being beaten up. Now that bitcoin is growing in popularity, you can move money anonymously, thus fueling crime and even dishonesty within families. Now anything can be done in secret, which makes everything depend upon human self-control and self-governing. How's that working for society?

11. Changing Values. I remember the intense discomfort when, as a youth, I heard the Rolling Stones' song Let's Spend the Night Together on our living room radio. My father was sitting in his familiar chair reading the Sunday paper—right there, in the same space with me, hearing the same lyrics I was hearing (or so I thought). I sat mortified, unable to think or move. And the lyrics continued: "Let's spend the night together/ Now I need you more than ever/ Let's spend the night together/ na, na, na." This scene is hardly understandable today. But in the late '60s and early '70s, Rock 'n' Roll stars like Jim Morrison of The Doors were arrested, sometimes only for profanity. Public intoxication and homelessness were illegal. Networks and the movie industry censored themselves to support values with which they thought the American people could identify. We are far from that world now.

12. Redefining "News." One must question the validity of the term "news," which most of us over the years have defined as "the facts about what happened today (or recently)." Of course, that's not what news programs present at all. Do programs offer objective news when we know huge amounts of money are paid in order to control what we see on the TV screen? What they tell you and how

they shape it will direct how and what you believe. And again, does it sensitize or desensitize, educate or manipulate? The ultimate freedom, as the author of Time Well Spent, Tristan Harris, said, is a free mind. We need a technology that's on our team to help us live, feel, think, and act freely. Unfortunately, those with political and economic power invest billions of dollars to counter free minds.

Tristan Harris, whose job title at Google was "design ethicist," has been an outspoken critic of how tech companies' products control our thinking. He says it is "the digital attention crisis" that is "hijacking our minds." He went on to say, "If you're an app, how do you keep people hooked? Turn yourself into a slot machine." The slot machine (driven by variable reinforcement) he refers to is the "pull down to refresh" mechanism on smart phones. It creates a repetitive demand that we update rather than miss something. It turns us into the mindless slot machine player, fixating his or her attention on the screen, all the while letting the world go by. He calls Facebook "a living, breathing crime scene." Did you know that Facebook derives its profits largely from the amount of time people spent interacting with the advertisements? They never want you to place your attention elsewhere. In effect, they don't want you to have a life. It costs them money.

And do you realize how reading a printed page is different from reading a screen? Many kids and adults today do not read from left to right, top to bottom. They look at a page or a screen searching for what is interesting or meaningful as they scan. Their eyes (and ours too) jump to the most attractive and dazzling images.

13. Are we the Eloi? Never before has society had this intense exposure to any content possible, easily acquired, just one button click away. We now check out eBooks from libraries without physically being there. But with all this power at our fingertips,

with all this knowledge and technological advancement, our world looks more and more like the dystopian visions of Orwell's 1984, Bradbury's Fahrenheit 451, or George Lucas's first film, THX 1138. The modern industrialized and digitized society bombards everyone with propaganda. Societies represented by these fictional works maintain that our free will is the enemy of happiness. Are we simply the Eloi walking trance-like to be enslaved and eaten by the Morlocks in H.G. Wells' The Time Machine? Are we the actors in a consumerism culture, paradoxically being consumed by it?

Suggested Solutions

Information is the defining attribute of the 20th and 21st centuries. The click of a button gives you access to information never realized by our ancestors, even as recently as 70 years ago. I've compiled several solutions to the problems that information introduces into our lives, and I'll share them with you here. These solutions come from a variety of sources, as well as from my own reasoning.

First, *we parents must make a decision to commit to dealing with the problems of media* in our own families. We must look at our own behavior. This may be the most difficult challenge of all in terms of screen control. How many of us often practice the same bad habits as our children? Do we check our iPad or iPhone compulsively, or whenever we hear an alert? Do we watch two hours of YouTube thinking only 20 minutes went by? Or do we lie next to our partner in bed, each texting or computing with little communication?

Many parents might be shocked to hear from their children how much parental screen time seems to interfere with family relationships. We know that modeling effects are powerful (the human impulse to copy others – think "role model"). Parents used to hide behind newspapers at the breakfast table, but now it is the screen interfering with eye contact, body language, attentiveness, and direct relationships. And unlike newspapers in the morning, our devices are with us almost around the clock – always ready to steal more of our attention. At least dad left the newspaper at home when he went off to work.

Children need to continually build social skills, the capacity for empathy and communication skills. They need to know how to present themselves, how to deal with conflict, and how to deepen friendships. We are the primary influencers of our children in all these skills. Social nuances are not easily picked up from a screen. There is no better place to teach necessary skills than the day-to-day exchanges among family members.

As parents, you have a great opportunity to model self-imposed limits. Let your children know how you limit what you watch or how you remain accountable to each other. Do NOT carry on a conversation while reading texts or texting or watching your device. Pause if you begin speaking to someone on a device if they don't turn to look at you. Be sure you reciprocate this so that when spoken to, you make eye contact and give attention.

We parents have a decision to make about our children's access to technology. We need to decide whether or not to allow our children televisions in their rooms and what programming they can access. Many parents decide to have television-free bedrooms, with one or two sets in other generally accessible rooms. If parents are watching something different in the living room, having another TV in a room that is not a bedroom would be one option. Having a TV in a child's room that is not connected to cable or the Internet is another possibility. Remember, television content is called 'programming' for a reason. It programs us purposefully to adopt someone else's values and to buy their products. Television programming secretly places hidden Trojan horse viruses within your and your child's "software," where it silently controls behaviors.

Consider your child's use of phones as well. The age at which to introduce phones and "screen time" is another important decision you must make. The American Academy of Pediatrics (AAP) recommends no screen time, except for video chatting, for babies up to 18 months. Furthermore, it suggests that parents limit preschoolers to an hour a day. For the younger child, limits are necessary to provide other experiences and interactions with the environment as their nervous system matures. Not until the early-to-mid-20s does essential neural development end. The AAP recommends plenty of "unplugged" time for face-to-face socializing, outdoor play, family activities, and sleep for older children. This is the other side of the seesaw for a balanced life. Time spent in face-to-face engagement in physical activities should far exceed screen time.

No eight-year-old needs to have a phone to call their parents to let them know their location (a parent actually said this was the reason her child was given a phone.) If you don't know where your eight-year-old is, that's a serious problem! Decide that unlimited time on screens is not good for developing children and probably not good for adults either. Talk to others, carry out research…yes, even on the internet.

There are many resources available for parents to find support and ideas for change. Make use of sites like Common Sense Media (commonsensemedia.org) to explore new ideas that will help you fashion a healthier balance of technology in the home. You might check out the work of Joe Edelman, a designer at the Center for Humane Technology. He's an insightful voice regarding the nature of social manipulation and digital design. Create informed limits that you think are reasonable within your family.

Second, *we must retrain ourselves and our children to create healthy habits* when engaging media in our homes. We need a balance between the digital and the person-to-person world. The only way we can achieve this balance is to be convinced it is necessary. Our awareness and thoughtfulness about structuring a healthy lifestyle – *our* lifestyle – propels us into action.

Awareness and commitment lead to options. To achieve this sought-after balance, many activities and interests are necessary. You should be wary of an isolated, sedentary life exemplified by this quip: My Internet was down for five minutes so I went downstairs and spoke to my family. They seem like nice people. But how do we create this balance?

The AAP encourages parents to create "sacred spaces." These locations or activities are screen-free so that conversation and other interests can emerge. Consider "prime" times for conversations, such as prior to breakfast, during meals (whether at home or in public), during the nightly bedtime routine, and short trips in the car. Live screens during these times actually serve to interfere and "triangulate" relationships with our children. As someone pointed out, you can offer your children something far more important during these "prime" times: you can give your attention. On longer trips in the car you can spark a dialogue or have the kids come up with a game to play. How about a round of "ask a question?" Many parents allow for more screen time during long trips, but perhaps the screens should not be the first thing offered.

But what about when we see our children using digital devices inappropriately? Don't pass up these experiences as teachable moments. If it is a personal wrong they do to another individual (i.e., bullying, sexting, inappropriate pictures, etc.), they also need to carry out the four-part forgiveness model when appropriate or possible. First, the offender says or writes in a single sentence what they did wrong, e.g., "I should not have sent those messages to you." Second, they make a commitment to fixing the problem behavior is in order, e.g., "I will work on only sending texts that are respectful." Third, they admit that the offended party is hurt by the behavior and ask for (not demand) forgiveness, e.g., "and I know I hurt you and hope when you work through your feelings, you could forgive me." The final step, if possible and appropriate, is to make amends to show the offending parties' seriousness. The child may do someone else's chores for two days or give the offended party $5-10.

Always look for teachable moments and honest communication with your children. Discuss what they think, what they've experienced, what they hear others experience, etc., to help them learn how they will navigate through the digital maze.

Regarding consequences for inappropriate use of digital devices, you may consider charging money or assigning more time doing extra chores. Be sure to make these consequences reasonable and logical, just as someone would pay extra when turning in a leased car with too many miles or returning a rented piece of equipment late. Over-punitiveness comes from a parent's anger, and a child will see through that. This s will lead to resentment, and will significantly interfere with the pedagogical impact. Whether in home school or traditional school, a problem behavior can and should lead to a learning experience.

But many teens now say that they are addicted to their screens and that the addiction interferes with their life. One solution, suggests Dr. Kathy Koch of Celebrate Kids, is a no-screen vacation. Another option is to agree that for one day, the family or maybe two people in the family will go without their screens so they can spend more time enjoying each other's company. We must always be conscientious of how screens can interfere with our relationships.

Listening well – no matter what the topic – and communicating our thoughts and feelings effectively are vital for good parenting. When speaking to your kids, especially teens, talk calmly, let them go first, show interest, and practice self-control when hearing things you find unpleasant. Avoid interrupting, and instead give empathy. Share your thoughts with no lectures. You can start by saying, "I want to run something by you and have you think about it." Or you can say, "I'd like your opinion. Tell me what you think tomorrow."

Be positive when talking to your child and come across like you believe kids can make wise choices just like wise adults do. As Jim Fay says, "There are a lot of bad things on the internet. The good news is that you're the kind of kid who can make smart choices about what you look at and what you don't." The point: have good expectations, even though we know kids will make some bad choices along the way...just as we did.

Another way to create healthy habits is to set aside quiet times and learn to become comfortable with boredom as an avenue to reflection and creativity. These times allow the imagination to be developed and cultivated. Creativity and creative thinking can flourish when you provide ample resources. Children can explore musical instruments, learn about mixing and recording equipment, develop drawing skills, create craft designs, build with blocks or construction toys, and so on.

The imagination can also be developed through physical play, which teaches many skills and expands a child's creativity. Some experts have called this "deep play" and those who share in it are "co-creators." Physical and occupational therapists tell us that physical play affects the inner ear, contributing to balance and self-awareness of how one's body reacts within the three-dimensional world. Physical exercise, as well as exercising the imagination, significantly and positively impacts our developing children.

Regularly initiate fun and imaginative activities with your children. Tell real stories from your lives. Make up stories where the adult starts and, after a short while, points to a child for them to continue the story. After a short while, the child points to another child or back to the parent. Have movie nights with your kids. Also, as kids get older, you may choose to watch a controversial movie and discuss the content and its effect on the watcher. Go to live events: plays, musicals, live music events, county fairs, etc. Have each person in the family take responsibility for planning one family activity and rotate each month. For example, have a fun family squirt gun fight in the backyard on a hot day.

Third, *we must learn how to safely engage with media* – to surf the web wisely – ensuring that media are always healthy sources of information and entertainment in our homes. We must do more than trust internet filters and screening software. While these safeguards are potentially useful, they are often ineffective and can be circumvented. Look for opportunities to help your children think through the wise use of these powerful digital tools. Just as we teach our children how to safely start a fire or how to safely sharpen a knife, or eventually, how to properly use a chainsaw, so too, we must teach digital competencies.

Have an occasional family meeting for just a few minutes to discuss what members think are healthy and reasonable guidelines for using digital devices. Have them articulate what they think are the benefits and underlying problems or dangers when using these powerful tools. We want to teach our children how to think, which is one of our primary goals in education. Our children need to learn how to assess for themselves the benefits, potential risks, and appropriateness of whatever comes their way.

Consider how to use media in specific areas of the house. Many families choose to have computers and tablets in rooms other than a child's bedroom. Computer screens should be positioned so that a passerby can easily see them. Limits, such as no phones in a child's room after eight o'clock, or some designated time prior to bedtime, are often useful. For young people growing up on phones, it is their lifeline, their source of oxygen, and their connection to the world. It is too tempting for them to respond when a friend texts them (and it would have been for us too if we had mobile phones in high school). As with anything, parents are responsible to model the values we teach.

Electronic game time is often limited within many families, sometimes causing a certain amount of frustration to parents if they are gamers themselves. Remember, showing your own self-prescribed limits will impact your kids and help you keep balance in your life as well. Also, as with the phone, require them to have an investment in some of the equipment. This is for several good reasons.

To foster the safe use of media at home, parents must have access to the child's permitted media accounts. Parents may also limit which apps are allowed. (When communication from someone on their phone often disappears after seconds, you may not have a way to scrutinize it. Those apps may be off-limits.) This, of course, runs into the legitimate issue of privacy. Yet the power of the internet and social media create a setting where the normal supervisory role of parents can easily be sidestepped. Good parents want to know who their child spends time with and what activities they engage in.

The internet and social media, for all their benefits, are turning the privacy issue on its head. Parents in a technologically-dominated world can no longer filter their children's social lives.

The new norm is for parents to have little knowledge of what parents need to know. So now, when parents attempt to gain back the knowledge they once had, it appears controlling and intrusive. Privacy in these digital days of parenting encourages more and more parental ignorance and lack of influence.

If you want your younger children to use mobile devices, make them "family" devices, controlled by parents and kept in a central location. It is much harder for parents to regulate time if the children think it's "their tablet." Also, significant reading needs to be done with real books. Forty-three percent of kids do not have a daily reading routine.

Our devices can also be extraordinarily important for our children's education. But children need to know how to use them safely and in a healthy manner. The devices can open communication between people and keep us in contact with others. They can be used for researching everything from how to tie a fishing knot to the current treatments for thyroid cancer. Make use of the many resources available, such as The Teaching Company Great Courses series, free online university course videos, iTunes U, and such things as free online music lessons. The list of valuable resources our digital devices can access is limitless. The internet even has sites with ideas about activities parents can do with her children without being online!

To monitor your children as they learn how to use their devices, you can enable the GPS function on our children's phones. As a parent, you need to have total access to the content of your child's phone, which makes sense until a certain age. Some families will be uncomfortable with invading their child's privacy, but for other families, it's like holding a young child's hand when walking along the sidewalk. We only let go of their hand when we're confident in their ability to walk along the sidewalk on their own. A child is vulnerable because they are often impulsive, and they have yet to learn how to judge the dangers of this world. A part of our job as parents is to help them develop judgment in navigating this world.

You can use parental controls as well as block or limit specific apps and features on your mobile devices. Blacklist or block specific content. Use whatever internet filtering services you can, but don't rely on them as a complete solution.

Many parents also choose a "basic" phone rather than a "smart" phone when providing a child with his or her first phone. Also, many parents decide that their child can participate in funding the phone to some degree, giving them a sense of responsibility over its care and use.

When giving an explanation to your children regarding limits placed on screens, you may wish to use the metaphor of eating proper portions or eating a broad range of healthy foods. You seek a variety of experiences for yourself and your family. When they complain, just say, "Yes, I know," avoiding long explanations. Save your breath. Don't offer long monologues on all the ways it might be bad for them.

But when it comes to bullying, we need to be models for our children. Practice what to do or say when they or someone else is bullied. Help them know how to think about the bully (they have issues!) and about themselves. (Feeling badly about yourself is losing the game. You are a good kid. You don't need to prove it.) Maybe as they see the bully as a sad, hurting kid, they may wish to pray for him or her. This frames the bully as someone for whom we should feel sorry, someone weak and needy, counteracting their perceived strength. Help your child know you have confidence in them to think and act to win the game. Practice rejection scenarios with your children. Make rejection a topic you can talk about easily. Point out that it's fairly common and that it's happened to you. "When someone rejects me, I like to think about the people who like me – my family and friends and the family dog." Prepare them how to think psychologically, if you will. "I just wonder what serious problems they must have to make them pick on others." Tell them how you think as a way of modeling the response.

Practice how to respond to online traps, just as we teach them how to respond to online bullies. Teach them what scam emails look like. Show them alternatives to clicking on links within emails. (If it shows a link to your checking account bank, open a new tab and type in the bank's name to go directly to it rather than through your email.) Let them know the wisdom of a position of skepticism when receiving emails from someone you do not know. That should be the norm. Skepticism. Also, teach them to never respond to emails that begin with "Hello," and then the first part of your email address. A company with whom you do business has your full name and will not address you improperly. On the internet, always think, "this could be anybody – be skeptical."

One important aspect of safely engaging with media is to reconsider how our children use non-structured time. Initially, if they already have bad habits with devices, they will almost certainly turn to their devices any free moment they get. But during this free time, give them plenty of things to play with, to build with, or to use during this time. As they explore and experiment, sprinkle in statements like, "You really worked hard on that even though it has been difficult," or "You must be pleased with yourself when you look at what you did."

Fourth, *directly confront and address the issue of inappropriate use of digital devices*. To deal with the porn problem, be sure you talk to your kids age-appropriately but explicitly about sexuality, its importance and power, its role in life, and how there are few things in life more powerful than sex. The more uninformed and naïve they are (and I'm not speaking of their innocence here), the more they will be ill-prepared to deal with pornography or bullying or even their own sexuality. Short discussions on several occasions will likely be much better than a single, long experience. How then should we as parents act when (not if) we discover our child has seen sexually explicit images/video/porn and/or extreme violence? Children are affected deeply by parental reaction to life events. Because they have an innate desire to win our approval, our behavior must be healthy and measured. The younger the child, the more likely they are to internalize our reaction as a statement about who they are. Bad parental reactions will only add to an already problematic event. So, do your best to be thoughtful and controlled, not reactive. Avoid an angry or judgmental response at all costs.

If you have a problem with your own emotions, tell your child you will discuss this important issue later. Give yourself time to calm down. Remind yourself how important your reaction is for your child. Then, and only then, should you address the issue. But it will be after you and your spouse or a good friend have discussed it.

It is important to keep in mind that our children will be exposed to violence, sex, etc., no matter what we do. They, just as we, are immersed in an information-saturated world where a few clicks can reveal any content that humans can imagine. So, we can only do our best to limit and screen inappropriate content. It is extraordinarily difficult to safely engage with media in today's world.

Remember, human beings are by nature curious, aggressive, and sexual. Even if you discover your child is intentionally looking at porn or violent videos, *never* communicate that you were shocked because a good child (or a godly child) would not want to do those things. *Never* say you are "so disappointed *in them*." The human trait of curiosity is often the thing that opens forbidden or unexplored doors. Ask yourself if you or a loved one ever slowed down to "rubber neck" as you drove by an automobile crash. Do not be unwittingly hypocritical.

Unfortunately, with humans, forbidden fruit is more attractive than what is permitted. Stolen water is sweet, as Proverbs says. We are all "tempted" by various things at various times. We all have yielded to temptation along the way. So be careful to keep your cool, avoid condemnation, and control your anxiety so that you can think clearly. Then have a proper discussion when the time comes.

Fifth, *we must be conscientious to change the way we think about media.* Don't raise an entertainment junkie. You do not have to keep them occupied and entertained every moment. In fact, that would be problematic. Children should relate to these phrases or words as they grow up: imagination, playing alone, playing with others, exercise, creative time, identifying and pursuing intrinsic interests. What gives them passion, curiosity, and interest? As one expert said, "Children who have been constantly entertained grow into adults who are constantly bored."

This chart shows the difference between entertainment and engagement. For most, engagement is the better of the two.

Entertained	Engaged
Mostly Passive	Mostly Active
Outside Stimulation	Internally Driven
Nonphysical	Physical
Reaction	Creation – Action
Manipulated	Manipulate
Defined Largely by Others	Self-Defined
Primarily Visual	Multidimensional

Entertained	Engaged
Dense and Fragmented (Rapid) Stimuli	Variable and Less Demanding Stimuli

As parents, it's important that we initiate what I call attitude or belief inoculation. Just as vaccines introduce a weakened form of a pathogen to develop anti-bodies to fight infection, so we as parents can use the same strategy to prepare our children for the coming social challenges. Talk with them rationally about a particular value or belief you wish them to keep. Then describe a common objection to that belief, helping them think through the issue, giving a counter argument where possible. For example, by giving a bit of the "virus" and developing a "belief antibody" in a controlled setting helps prepare them when other values are expressed out there in "the world." You don't want them confronted with a strong argument against a core value having never thought it through, with no cognitive defenses. It even helps you as a homeschooling parent to have well-thought answers to the common questions coming your way, such as "What about socialization?"

At the same time, we must put media and technology in their proper places in our lives. We must set limits, not only for our children, but for ourselves. Allow notifications from people, not machines. Notifications keep our phones vibrating to lure us back into apps that are unnecessary.

Limit your first page of apps to just tools— things you use for in-and-out tasks like Maps, Camera, Calendar, Notes, or Lyft. Move the rest of your apps off the first page and into folders.

Then launch other apps by swiping down to type the app you want. Typing takes just enough effort to cause us and our children to pause and ask, "Do I really want to do this?"

Say "yes" to the outdoor or tabletop games your kids want to play. Find games that appeal to children and parents alike. Find a special non-video game you and your spouse can play.

Use a separate alarm clock in your bedroom and charge your phone in another room (or on the other side of the bedroom.) This way, you can wake up without getting sucked into your phone before you even get out of bed. When we wake up in the morning and turn our phone over to see a list of notifications, it frames our experience of "waking up in the morning" around a menu of "all the things I've missed since yesterday." (For more examples, see Joe Edelman's Empowering Design talk.) So, practice the 10-10 or the 15-15 principle: make the decision that these first minutes after awakening and the first minutes you arrive home will be screen free. Do your best to avoid consuming visual news programs and stick to text-based ways of getting information regarding current events.

Some parents realize the difficulty in changing "TV addiction." A parent complained of having no free time, but when they and their spouse decided to put all TVs in the garage for one year, he suddenly had hours each evening that he did not realize he wasted in front of the television. He also said astonishingly, "It took me a while to figure out how to use that time! I wasn't sure what to do." Other families have disconnected from satellite or cable, relying on other services such as Netflix and Hulu. If families insist on watching local news, inexpensive digital antennas can be purchased for local stations without having 100 channels of TV wasteland.

Two things to remember: kids have texting shorthand to communicate things that parents may not understand and that contribute to secrecy. Quick texting of a few letters can alert their friends that parents are in the room, or conversely, when parents have exited. Second, kids can use cloaking apps and other ways to hack their device in order to hide things from you.

Understanding the psychology of your children helps you look for practices that, regardless of the content, avoid creating unnecessary resistance. Rather than posting private family photos online to share with friends and family, instead create a private Dropbox folder or Facebook group just for people you choose to share with. This way, all your precious, private family memories will stay within the confines of your own household, as opposed to posting to a broader, perhaps unknown, group of people who may not even know you or your children.

In this chapter, I have laid out various ways to create healthy boundaries in the use of media and technology in our homes. Given the prevalence of media and the ease in using technology, some of the solutions I've outlined won't be easy. But with conscientiousness and diligence we can make positive changes in our families as we live in a rapidly changing, technical world.

Chapter 4 Application

1. How are your children's lives different from yours at their age? What are examples of the speed of change in the world and how can this rapid change affect us?

2. What is your relationship to digital devices and social media? After reading this chapter, what pleases you about your use of technology and what do you think you should change, if anything? What worries you?

3. How should you as a parent deal with invisible (cloaked) apps that your child can have on their phone, tablet, or computer that you may never know are there?

4. How did you or will you talk to your children about what their friends or acquaintances might do with their technological devices? What kinds of choices will your children have as they interface with others in our digital world? Ask them what they have seen or heard on others' devices as well as their own. Is there anything that made them uncomfortable? Anything gross? Anything having to do with bodies or nakedness or sexual stuff? Find out in a nonreactive way.

5. The Bible tells us not to love the world and not to be manipulated by it. What could this mean? Consumerism? Greed? Hatred? Prejudice? Injustice? Smoking? Discuss.

6. Look at how you and your family do or don't do selfies or constant photography. Could this be narcissistic in some cases? Are you fully present in family experiences when you are fumbling

with your phone and posing? Is there a way to be fully present in family experiences and still at times, take selfies?

Take pictures but maybe fewer pictures. Experience those who are with you and avoid the temptation to impress others on social media with exciting pictures of your exciting life. We need to be fully present, living authentic lives.

7. What techniques do the "news" shows use in order to keep you watching and to keep you coming back? Which techniques are designed to promote strong uncomfortable feelings in the viewer? What do you think of this and how will you help yourself and your children avoid having their "programming" manipulate and restrict how you think?

8. How do children express anxiety or worry? Why would kids worry these days and what should a parent do if their child is overly anxious?

9: If you have a choice, get your daily dose of current events from the printed texts rather than visual images. Do you think there are significant differences in effects between the printed word and the live feed, video world? Discuss this and contemplate deciding about whether you want to thoughtfully steer yourself more to the written word than the video images.

Chapter 5: Why Emotional Growth Takes So Long

"Our character is but the stamp on our souls of the free choices of good and evil we have made through life."

-Geikie

Michael and Steve found a cocoon in the yard. The butterfly had the cocoon opened at the top and was struggling to get out of it to fly away.

The two boys watched the struggle for a long time. Their compassion for the butterfly was so great that they gently tore the cocoon apart so the butterfly could be free to fly away.

They pulled the butterfly out of his cage and gently placed him on the ground. The butterfly's wings were shriveled and still.

The boys ran home to their dad for help. After some research, the boys learned that in their attempt to help the butterfly fly, they had made it impossible for him to fly. Monarch butterflies can take hours of struggle to be freed from their cocoons. But that process is important for the development of its wings. The struggle itself sends fluid to the wings and gives them the strength they need to carry the butterfly in the air.

The two boys, empathizing with the animal's struggle, could only envision the final outcome of the butterfly flying. They were ignorant of the important process the butterfly had to go through in order to fly at all. In this same way, we must not be ignorant of the developmental processes our children need to experience to be strong adults. Our feelings for them must not cause us to prevent them from experiencing normal life.

A related topic discussed in home school circles is the developmental view of education. The word "develop" means to grow, to unfold or expand gradually and in stages; the process from earlier to later stages of maturation. This all seems harmless enough. I have read or heard of statements from home school leaders such as "I'm not a developmentalist... I take a biblical view," or "A developmental approach is what behaviorists take and they are humanistic." At this point, I usually start muttering how I will write my congressmen to pass a law against this kind of wildly incorrect speech.

The Bible is full of developmental examples and themes. The very creation shouts out that there are stages of maturation through which animal and plant life progress. Infants, while totally human, are not little adults. Adults are not oversized children. Saint Paul uses this obvious truth to illustrate an unfolding of understanding in the Christian life when he refers to the milk and the meat of the Word (I Cor. 3:2). Paul also makes it clear that while all Christians are equally going to heaven, only those who have been believers for some time (possessing signs of maturity) should be in positions of authority in the local church (I Tim. 3:2).

God Himself unfolded His plan and truth to people over the ages. The disciples were shown truths over time and on many levels (e.g. the teaching technique of parables.) Their understanding grew, not just in the amount of what they knew but the quality. Their ability to use the knowledge matured as well. There is a spiritual development that progresses as a believer slowly moves from being a "babe in Christ" to a person established in the faith. All the books and sermons in the world cannot make one instantly wise.

This is one reason the "gray headed ones" are to be respected according to the Bible (Prov. 16:31).

Maturity requires time and experience with God and life. It requires understanding at lower levels to be able to grapple with more complex levels. Spiritual development truly encompasses the whole person and has to do with relating to God and fulfilling our role in the kingdom of God.

There are even things God hides about Himself or does not expose us to in its fullness because we can't handle it (His power being one of them.) He gives us pieces and glimpses that are appropriate, lest we be consumed.

Jean Piaget, the famous Swiss child researcher, observed that children move though predictable stages of cognitive and intellectual development. Giving a college lecture to an infant (in the sensory-motor phase) who learns by sensation and putting things in his mouth will obviously fail. You teach an infant about the building blocks of life thorough sensory experience (something appropriate to his stage of development.) Similarly, you don't talk about abstract theological concepts when you are doing child evangelism. It doesn't work either. What you do is go to a flannel board and show concrete examples to illustrate a simple story.

Lawrence Kohlberg and others have concluded that moral development also moves through definable stages in children. We also see in normal growth a movement from external reasons for right behavior (I will get caught) to an internal control (it is wrong).

Physical development certainly is marked by stages of readiness and ability. Trying to teach certain physical skills such as an infant holding its head up will fail until the neuromuscular pathways are established that allow for this operation. This readiness must be considered if proper care and teaching will take place. One popular writer asked, "Would you stop using diapers for an eight-month-old child? If not, then you are a developmentalist."

Social maturation certainly progresses through stages. Relating to parents provides a first understanding of what a relationship is; then comes the task of relating to same sex children and later, relating to the opposite sex. You must accomplish one task before moving on. If you believe that there are age appropriate things to talk about and age appropriate behaviors (for instance, kids don't date when they are twelve years old), then you believe in a developmental understanding of people.

Researcher and secular psychologist David Elkind, in his book *The Hurried Child*, and its sequel, *All Dressed Up and No Place to Go*, advocates a return to the readiness principle. He shows persuasively how modern culture treats children like little adults and expects a precocity that is dangerous and damaging. (He puts home schoolers down in this early work because he mistakenly thought parent educators were all ignoring readiness, doing flash cards and pushing academics with three-year-olds, trying to make super-kids.)

One of the main arguments for homeschooling is that public and private schools usually fail to consider the developmental stages of the individual child, especially in classrooms where differences cannot be truly appreciated. Taking the time and giving individual attention based upon the stage of learning of the student is not usually possible. Home education allows for these differences.

Review your parenting style. Do you consider your children's various stages of spiritual, physical, cognitive, and moral maturation? Do you realize they don't see the world like you do and that their view is normal for their age?

With your children, are you interested in more than just good behavior? Do you see mistakes and even misbehavior as part of the process of learning or an impediment to learning? Are you more concerned about self- directed good behavior in those youngsters or just simply right behavior so that everything is in place? Do you think of your children as natural learners or think that they must be made to learn?

Think about your curriculum. Is its primary thrust understanding or simply memorizing in order to give the right answer on the test? Is it flexible enough to allow for differences or is it forcing every child to a rigid set of academic expectations that use an adult learning model? How do you use your curriculum? Are you adaptive and teaching to the student or are you enslaved to the directions in the book, having to do every problem on every page?

Review your expectations of yourself. Are you a learner who is maturing or are you supposed to have it all together? Can you have bad days, good days, effective days, and ineffective days?

When we understand and accept a developmental view of life and learning, we help our children feel normal. When we don't, we are using a model and guide for life that is not true and not biblical. Trouble will be forth- coming. Your expectations will be incorrect and so will your children's. A traveler will eventually get lost if he has an inaccurate map, even though early in the journey he won't know it.

Shallow and non-developmental models of personality turn people away from how God has made us. Therefore, children's behavior and more importantly, their deepest selves, can be damaged. Fruit must grow from flowering to ripening. Each stage has different needs.

Think developmentally as you work with your child, striving to know him and meet his needs.

Chapter 5 Application

1. Have you experienced stages of development in your child's life such as the independent two-year-old or the magical thinking of the five-year-old? How would developmental stages impact your teaching and parenting?

2. Have you experienced readiness in your child physically, emotionally, or intellectually? How does this impact your teaching and parenting?

3. What damage could be done by ignoring stages of development or readiness?

Dr. Dale Simpson

Chapter 6: Teaching Your Children to Fail

"What is defeat? Nothing but education; nothing but the first step to something better."

- Wendell Phillips

Trying to help his wife, Chad inadvertently ended civilization as we know it when he placed the bowls where the cups go in the dishwasher.

Teaching your children to fail? There must be a typographical error. Aren't we in the business of success and excellence and doing the right things? Aren't we who believe in the Christian faith in search of excellence?

Some time ago, my wife saw our then 8-year-old son outside with his 6-year-old brother. The 8-year-old was riding his bike in front of his brother and then jumping off into the dirt. When she asked him what he was doing, he replied, "Michael wants to learn how to ride a bike, so I'm teaching him how to fall the right way." Our 8-year-old knew that falls were in his brother's future, so he set out to prepare him.

One of the most important lessons you can teach your children is how to fail. Actually, they already know how to fail, but our job is to teach them how to fail with a healthy and godly attitude.

We live in a digital world where all blemishes are removed from the final print. Because families are mobile and more private than in the past, we just see the outer skin of others' lives and rarely glimpse at their frailties. All too often, failure is still seen as an enemy that must be defeated. But real life suggests that making mistakes is an inevitable part of our human existence, and we must prepare our children for a proper understanding of its place in the Christian life.

Look at your reaction when you fail. Do you want to announce it to the world? I doubt it. Like the saying goes, "Everyone likes to be noticed, but no likes to be stared at." What takes place inside of you when your child knocks something over or spills something? Is it often as if he did something on purpose? Frequently, there is a lot of shame imbedded in this process. Somehow children think they are bad if they mess up. This is the part we parents want to eliminate. People are not bad for making mistakes. Mistakes are just seemingly an inconvenience.

Too many of us have strong emotional reactions, particularly anger, when others make mistakes. This reaction is not only directed outward, but frequently is the same reaction that we have internally to our own mistakes and shortcomings. In their most fundamental sense, these reactions reflect a ready frustration and hostility when circumstances don't go just according to our plan.

How is it that we react to mistakes and failures with indignation? Often, it seems to us that the person making the mistake has done something willful and of a particularly personal nature to us. Where do these reactions come from and how do we want our children to react to our failure or the failures of their children?

Mistakes are not the same things as sins. Too often we parents react to mistakes with moral outrage. We must remember that sin is a willful disobedience to God. It has nothing to do with an accident or ignorant behavior. Sin at its core is rebellion against God's way rather than a mistake. If we are going to teach our children a proper response to mistakes, we must separate these kinds of failures and shortcomings from sin and a theological response.

Shame is not the same as guilt. Healthy guilt feelings are remorseful emotions we feel over an immoral act or the failure to act in some moral way. But guilt feelings can accompany a guilty act or they can occur when nothing morally wrong has happened.

We may feel morally guilty over something for which we are not guilty. Conversely, we may not feel guilty over things that are blatant sin. Guilt feelings over something we are not guilty of could be called neurotic guilt feelings. The deep feeling of worthlessness as a person is called shame. St. Paul calls misplaced guilt or shame worldly sorrow" in II Cor. 7:8-10, and contrasts it to godly sorrow which "leads to life, repentance, and a clear conscience."

Worldly sorrow or shame creates a crushing feeling that attacks the very sense of self. Dr. James Dobson calls this breaking the spirit, and it has nothing to do with genuine conviction, though it masquerades as such. Ironically, shame does not lead to change and repentance but rather to some form of internal defense and denial. Healthy guilt feelings lead to confession and change.

James 1: "The anger of man does not accomplish the righteousness of God."

What then do we do regarding mistakes and shortsightedness that occur in our children's lives?

1) Stay in control of our own emotions and act towards it just like we would any other thing we don't like but must live with.

2) Allow reasonable consequences to occur so that both learning and some restitution will result. For example, if a child leaves a tool out in the rain and the tool rusts and is no longer useful, the child will be asked to purchase a new tool — or if it's extremely expensive, some part of the tool's cost. An alternative might be for the child to help oil and repair the tool while other children are playing so that it is restored to its original function.

Spanking or other forms of discipline which imply that the behavior was willful should never be applied to a mistake. Another example would be a child reaching for a glass on a high shelf in the kitchen, only to accidentally have it shatter at her feet. A reasonable consequence would be that the child help clean it up. If the child is too young, then after the parent cleans it up, the child could carry the bag to the garbage can. No scolding or spanking or other forms of discipline should be used because it would miss the point of the behavior. In this way, the natural flow of life occurs in the same way it occurs to adults. We lick our wounds and reasonable consequences are applied.

3) Cultivate a view of failure as simply another teaching moment. There is a story of a project manager for a multinational corporation who, having completed an assigned task, lost the company one million dollars. His boss called him in for what the manager was sure to be his unceremonious firing. The boss then

presented him with a new twenty-million-dollar project to supervise. The surprised man accepted the challenge, saying, "I have to be honest, I thought you were going to fire me." The boss retorted, "Fire you! When I've just spent one million dollars to train you?"

What we do not want to do is to react to failure out of anger, shaming the child or asking why and showing we are really upset with him. This accomplishes nothing positive. All it will do is to further make the child hide his mistakes from the parent rather than help him to prevent mistakes. The child will also internalize our rage at him so he develops a strong sense of shame and "badness" when messing up. He will project this to others' mistakes at a later date and pass the tradition down.

After mistakes, we want to offer brief, appropriate instructions only if the child does not appear to know how to accomplish the task. Mistakes are often the result of not paying attention to the task-- a task they generally understand. Saying little is the best approach.

Any emotional baggage in the parent can push them to err with either too harsh a response or too little if they always mop up for a child's mistakes in areas he can help fix. Parental anger and rage reflect a childlike temper tantrum on the parent's part and is unhealthy. Too little of a response presents a model for living that is unrealistic since that is not the way life will be outside of the home.

Teaching our children how to handle failure is an exciting part of parenting and one that will be entirely useful for them throughout their lives. Furthermore, God will get the most out of their lives when they are willing to take managed risks with themselves and not be afraid of bold attempts at accomplishing certain goals. People who are shame-based and are afraid of failure tend to be overly cautious in tackling life head-on. They tend to wait for only the tasks that appear one-hundred-percent likely to succeed. These people are not front-line soldiers in life. They sit back waiting for someone else to hit the beach and tell them everything is okay.

Surely not all people can be leaders, but we don't want to overly inhibit our children just because of our angry reactions. Let's pass on a legacy that teaches the difference between sin and mistakes. Let's eliminate crushing shame as a response to failure in our children. Ensure that your kids know how to fail — the right way.

Chapter 6 Application

1. How was failure handled in your family as you grew up?

2. How do you react to your failures? Your children's failures?

3. Is there anyone in your child's life who is overly critical of failure? Is there anyone in your child's life who minimizes failure, trying to cover it up out of sympathy?

Dr. Dale Simpson

Chapter 7: Helping the Troubled Child

"Man is born into trouble as surely as sparks fly upward."

- Job 5:7

It was a long 14 years, but Tommy had learned his lesson about hitting his sister.

"This wasn't supposed to happen," said one anguished parent. "They've been homeschooled all their lives and have always been good kids. How could they be so rebellious and go against what they've been taught?" For many, parenting the home school child has become difficult and quite disillusioning. They didn't expect to have these kinds of symptoms and problems in a child's life if they "did the right thing by homeschooling." How can children, raised with all the promises of home school socialization and its emphasis upon instilling godly values, go astray in later years?

For most home school parents, homeschooling is an exciting opportunity to participate in their children's education. For most, it is also a wonderful way to accomplish many of the emotional and developmental goals we have for our children. Parents read with enthusiasm articles and books describing how successful homeschooling can be accomplished. They read how socialization is improved, and how the more extreme values in a hedonistic world can be stopped from dominating children's lives.

Many parents are excited that healthier, restrained, godly values can be built into their child's lives. Many homeschooling parents see home education and its emphasis upon family life as a promise to avoid the painful experiences they themselves went through in their youth. With this early optimism, some parents find themselves in disbelief and shock when their older child becomes troubled.

More and more parents are in pain over a troubled child in the home school family. Paralleling this pain is the embarrassment and shame these parents often feel when they're in their home school or church group. Parents tell me that they feel awkward and uncomfortable around others, often feeling condemned or judged because of their child's behavior. The teen who shows up with a nose ring or a tattoo can be quite disconcerting to the little home school co-op group who meets every Friday. That child can quickly become the focus of other children's attention ranging from ire to envy. This can have a ripple effect upon other families and present challenges for those parents.

Troubling behavior can occur in home-schooled children for a number of reasons. First, home education is not a panacea or magical activity that guarantees a desired outcome.

Unfortunately, some things published in the home school community sound like there is an ironclad guarantee that if you do certain things with your children, great things will always be accomplished. These expectations tend to be naive at best, and a piece of marketing at worst.

We should understand that fearful parents tend to grasp hold of formulas and methods which promise to meet the wishes of the parents. The more fearful a parent is, the more they may convince themselves of the certainty of a particular method. This, of course, helps quiet the parents' anxiety, but it leaves them vulnerable to heartbreak and disappointment if the method they are clinging to falls short. You can see this in how people tenaciously hold onto the words of certain Christian leaders as if they are gospel.

Some leaders in the Christian world have set up elaborate systems that they ask you to follow with the promise that if you throw your life into it, things will come out the right way. It is my experience that these parents are often rigidly holding onto the leader's perspective and therefore are not as adaptable or teachable in their parenting. Then when the symptoms emerge in the teen, either the teen is blamed or the parents feel disillusioned and rudderless. They become rudderless because they have been taught for years that all the other systems are bad, and they are following the only right way. When their "true" system fails, they have no place to turn. Our over-dependence upon any model can lead to the inability to adapt.

The second reason why problems can occur in children is that children have a will and make choices. No matter how good the environment, as important as this is, people still make choices to pursue things that are sometimes not good for them. Fortunately, children with a good foundation almost always come back eventually, although it may be with a few scars.

Third, the teen years quickly expose any need for the parent to control a child. The model says that we are primarily consultants to our children rather than commanders or rescuers. The goal for our children is self-controlled, good behavior. We are not looking for dominated people who act well when they are around us but are out of control when they leave. As children age, the culture affords them more and more opportunity to act and think differently than their parents.

Care must be taken by the parent not to engage in power struggles and to carefully assess their own motivation. Parents should look deeply within themselves and ask, "Am I doing things with my children based upon my fears and my need to reduce my fears rather than helping equip them to manage their lives well?" Of course, there are things to be afraid of, but we need to look at our method of interaction with our children and ask, "Am I trying to control something outside of myself so that I can control my fearful insides?" "Have my children complained that I'm trying to control them and could they be right?"

Another variant of control finds parents adopting a need to teach, manage, and instruct others. Many women have been placed in the "parental child" role from their family of origin and continue in it even as adults. These parents need to be sure that everything works out right, otherwise they would feel guilty that they are not doing their jobs. While this may appear to work fine when you are dealing with self-control, trying to control others and make certain their choices work out right can cause problems. Compulsive helping is still compulsive, and it's not usually helping.

For many parents it is difficult to separate their role as parent from their child's choices. It is for some folks a difficult thing to avoid feeling guilty when their child makes a poor choice. The reasoning goes, "If I were a good parent, they would not think or act that way." Therefore, when parents see a child thinking or acting in the wrong way, they take it upon themselves to change it and fix the child so that they can feel like a better parent. This, of course, can lead to more power struggles and can exaggerate the troubled behavior. Remember, good kids from good families think and choose badly sometimes.

A fourth reason for troubled behavior is that adolescence in our culture is a difficult period. My observation is that it is difficult in this culture for teens to demonstrate consistent faith and spirituality. There are certainly stellar examples of apparent teen maturity. But it is simply difficult to be an adolescent, exist in the world, and not be largely affected by it.

As mentioned earlier, one of our parenting goals is attitude inoculation. We don't hide our children in every way from the world, but we can help them be aware of the world and the emotional and spiritual issues. Some parents are still shocked that their kids would care about some of the things in modern culture, and they react poorly when their children show interest in such things. Parents can shame a child just for being drawn to something. This confuses attraction with misbehavior, feelings with sin, and healthy guilt feelings with shame. This can exaggerate symptoms and help inflame the child's need to establish himself as different from his parents. The mistakes a parent can make here are either disinterest or control. Let's be active yet careful in our parental guidance as we negotiate the cultural mine field.

Troubled behavior in children can sometimes be a symptomatic reaction to other family issues. For instance, introducing two foster children into the family will create major changes. Financial setbacks that require significant adjustments in a family can also affect children. Fathers who have had a rather distant and uninvolved relationship can, by the teen years, be written off in the child's mind. Other groups become replacements for the attention of a father. Marital problems, mid-life crises and other issues within the family could be creating conflicts that are acted out by the troubled child. Care should always be taken to do a family assessment before quick conclusions about the individual child are drawn.

Another reason for troubled behavior could be called the "Alcohol, Drugs, Romance Factor." Kids who are otherwise fairly decent, when under the influence of chemicals including their own hormones, can show radical changes in behavior. When someone has become infatuated or "in love" with another (especially if it has a sexual component, symptoms usually appear. These symptoms may be seen in anger towards parents, leaving and not asking permission, staying out late and even, for some older kids, staying away from home two or three days at a time. These symptoms are loud statements about the seductiveness and the power of drugs or infatuation in the lives of human beings. Care must be taken to see beyond and beneath the symptomatic behavior and to find the real issues while at the same time not indulging misbehavior.

Another contributor to misbehavior is seen when some kids reflect their rebelliousness toward parents in a rebellious choice against God. They may be spiritually shaking their fist at God and not wanting any of the healthy self-control that God demands. God gets linked to their issues with mom and dad. Duty and responsibility can seem to them like control, a prison sentence, or "things children do." For sure, their fight sometimes is with God. At other times, their fight with God is really an extension of their perceived fight with us.

A few weeks ago, two of my teens attended a large teen weekend rally billed as a time for getting serious with God to challenge the teens in their Christian walk. There were a number of things the kids enjoyed, but when it came down to the real focus of the evening by the adult leader, it became a high-pressure appeal for money. After that was laid on the kids, there was heavy emphasis on raising money to go on their particular mission trips. This is the kind of ridiculous, controlling behavior that many adults attempt with teenagers. Unfortunately, teens will often superficially respond to this because many of them are troubled and guilt ridden. Teens will frequently do whatever it takes to keep more guilt off their shoulders. To be sure, teens under real conviction by God's Spirit, can and do respond to mission trips and challenges to their Christian walk. But I would submit that parents in general, and sometimes homeschooling parents in particular, have more of a need to control their children than they are willing to admit or than they are aware of. The parents may feel it is their Christian duty to be sure the child does not misbehave or they may, in a more dysfunctional way, experience a child as an extension of themselves. Poor personal boundaries lead to poor consequences.

In any case, home school parents should be on the lookout for their own need to control and be sure to address these issues early in their child's development. Troubled kids need their attention focused on their own behavior, the consequences, and the difficult decisions they will make. They don't need confused boundaries and power struggles with their parents to cloud the issue.

Parents of troubled kids can make the common mistake of avoiding their difficult child because that is the parent's style of handling conflict or because the parents finally get so frustrated they know of no more options in relating. This can be a difficult line to walk when a child is not responsive to the parent and the parent needs to show emotional engagement while not controlling the child. This engagement without attacking or running away is the position to seek.

One of the things that can sometimes help keep the relationship engaged is the frank and timely confession by the parents that they are sad over the state of the relationship and that they would like to see it better. This drops down to the deeper issues and avoids the important, but nonetheless more superficial issues that we end up having conflict over such as dress, going out at night, etc. If this is said without implying that the child has messed up the relationship but rather saying that the parents grieve over the current state of the relationship, possible points of contact can be made. Then ways to make things better or activities to share could be brain- stormed until at least one idea surfaces.

Care must be taken at this stage not to yield to the temptation of arguing the more surface issues as the child throws them out in response to your statement about the relationship. Responding to "If you'd just let me go to that night club and leave me alone" is tempting but the wise parent will avoid responding directly to that. "I know we have some differences about how wise it is for you to go to that place, but I would rather talk about the conflict this has created between us and about how we're not feeling close in our relationship" would be one possible response.

Showing genuine sadness and concern without trying to manipulate or control your troubled child will give you a chance to connect. This connection is vital so that when the day comes that true insight and perhaps brokenness occur, you will be emotionally ready to welcome home your prodigal son.

Chapter 7 Application

1. What situations in your parenting are motivated by fear for your child? Does this fear lead to clear thinking or reacting? How can you take time to "think" in these situations rather than "react"?

2. Do you think that if your child makes wise choices, you are a good parent? If your child makes a foolish choice, do you think you are a bad parent?

3. In what instances can you be secure enough to discuss alternative views of your values without fear?

Dr. Dale Simpson

Chapter 8: A Call to Action

"Think like a man of action, act like a man of thought."

- Henri Louis Bergson

There must be some kind of epidemic going around. You know, some virus quietly infecting the planet that will someday bring an end to civilization as we know it. Perhaps you've seen the effects of it where you live. I have. I see it in shopping malls, doctor's offices, in theaters and churches.

The victims? It apparently strikes adults with children. The symptoms? These adults are stricken with a certain mental and behavioral paralysis that renders them helpless to intervene to get children under control. Children can be dismantling the office furniture or shouting, "I want my toy back!" and the helpless victim ignores it as if it is not real. Some less infected individuals try to reason or bargain with the offending child, thinking this helps in keeping the peace. I've seen adults bribe children with gifts or promised activities if they will stop yelling and carrying on. It's amazing. Someone needs to call the Center for Disease Control so they can work on an antidote. Maybe they can reduce the risk of infection by teaching "safe parenting." Society is crumbling when parents are mental hostages to children.

How will our society survive when these undisciplined children become parents? These are the next generation of voters who will decide how a government should act. We are quickly becoming a people given to impulse and lack of inhibition. Many children are not taught to see and accept the reality of others' needs and sensibilities. Some parents are raising a generation of individuals who have never learned to say "no" to themselves.

I like parents... most of the time. But I want to scream when I hear a child talk disrespectfully to her parents while the parent impotently tries to reason with her.

Could this problem be happening in home school families? Yes. We have our share of this affliction in the form of passive, insecure parents who often don't know how to be a solid person to their children. They may get pushed to a level of yelling or over-action, but they fail to know how to be firm with junior early enough in a behavioral sequence to help the child learn to say no to the impulses. I know a few well-meaning, loving parents who simply don't see how they let their children dominate and define family events. These parents usually grow in their frustration with their child (others are often more frustrated with the children) and feel increasingly helpless to get the youngster in control. They often respond to advice with "We tried that...it just doesn't do any good with Billy."

Why Do Parents Give In?

At least five reasons come to mind that explain why some parents cannot be firm with their children.

1. They don't feel comfortable with their own parental power.

2. They feel guilty about not being around their children enough and become conflicted when they have to say no.

3. They have learned passive coping mechanisms that value avoiding a problem over confronting a problem.

4. They are too emotionally needy to make the child's supervision the most important thing to pursue at that time.

5. They have rejected certain parenting methods they experienced growing up.

The consequences of this overly passive pattern include:

a) Other people become frustrated and angry at the passive parents and their offspring.

b) The child fails to learn consistent inner controls of impulses.

c) The child learns to interpret restrictions on his desires as abnormal or unnatural.

d) The child feels alone and detached from the interpersonal world around him.

The model of parenting presented here promotes two themes. It offers consistent, unconditional affirmation of the child along with consistent, reasonable application of limits and structure so self-control can be learned. On the limits and structure side, we are trying to help the child move from external control ("If you jump up and down on the chair you will have to sit in my lap") to partial internal control ("I want to jump on the chair but I won't because others don't like it and I could get in trouble") to full internal control ("I want to jump on the chair but I don't want to damage things that should be treated carefully").

A few tasks necessary to achieve mature behavior are impulse control, social etiquette, and learning how to respect others' feelings as much as your own (empathy). These tasks are supported by loving and consistent limits set by the parent in the early years. More structure and direct supervision are needed in the earlier years so that later, the child can exercise self-control as he experiences less control by parents. So often, the American family does it the opposite way, tightening down with more controls as the teen years grow after having few controls early on. This produces power struggles and is a losing battle. Controlling a teen is harder than controlling a younger child. Besides, we want our children to learn to control themselves.

What Are Some Practical Things Parents Need to Keep in Mind?

1. Physically restrain, hold, or move two or three-year-olds rather than just using words to direct them. Words and reasoning don't work well by themselves with younger ones. Words must be paired with structure and experience.

Dad is reading the newspaper and notices three-year-old Megan pulling the cat's ears. "I don't want you to pull the cat's ears and tail because cats don't like it and you pulled his ears last time and he scratched you, and cats are more docile and are rather independent and Daddy really likes that cat so I don't want you to..." Ugh! Action must replace verbiage. Move the child or hold her. Expect the child to have desires to pull the cat's ears. Just teach her that she can experience frustration of that impulse and still survive. Avoid yelling or threats.

2. Have clear school time rules that may be more structured than other "around the house" rules. This can help things be less chaotic during school time and it helps the child learn there are different occasions for behavior.

3. Ask your children to have an "inside voice" (inside a house vs. outside in the great outdoors) when around others. Voice volume is a learned function. Parents who raise loud, dominant children have alternatives. I'm not including here the totally busy, clinically hyperactive child whose motor is running without a governor. These kids can be managed but are not the same as kids whose parents have just gone deaf when they yell. Some parents keep responding to a child when the child is being loud and demanding. This is a mistake. All movement toward what the child wants should stop when they are whining, loud, etc. The key is to teach children to talk in a reasonable voice around others or in a public place. Many passive parents raise kids you hate to stand near in the grocery line.

4. Don't be afraid to use your lap and arms to help a child gain control. When young children, for example, hit parents because they are frustrated at a limit, parents do the child great disservice when they ignore or laugh it off. Holding children until they yield to the grown up (sometimes out of their own exhaustion) has its place in the parenting of young children. Always be careful in physical expressions with children. Do not use grabbing or physical control at all on post puberty children unless you are protecting self or others. Any physical threat of violation is perceived differently after puberty. Avoid sudden snatching or grabbing any aged children just because you are frustrated.

5. Be careful not to engage in debate or lengthy explanation. This explaining is usually something you are doing for you; to make you feel better and lessen your guilt feelings in setting a limit with your child. Parents often talk as if waiting for junior to validate and agree with them. It's really okay to have a different view of things than your children. It's okay if a child experiences disappointment.

6. Realize that one of your jobs as parent is to shape behavior and to teach what works and doesn't work in the world. Avoid the following scenario that I overheard with a home school family: The four-year-old was hitting the glass window in the family van with a metal object. Mom said, "Don't hit the glass... it will break." The child proceeded to hit the glass and mom ignored it. Later she came back and told him again not to hit the glass, while explaining that it would break, only to continue to remain inactive with the child. This continued on and off for quite some time. What a sad commentary on a parent's inability to be an adult around a four-year-old. How awful it must be to feel intimidated by a child. How awful for the child to know his parents are much weaker than he is.

Even though I am emphasizing action and control, don't forget the other things in child rearing that are important. Gentleness, sensitivity, and support of the choosing child are elements of good parenting, too. These gifts to our children are also active, not passive. They are not the result of us being inadequate in our role as authority. We must be comfortable with our position as benevolent authority. This helps children feel secure and gives them a social environment where they can learn to control the screaming impulses within them. If done early in life, this will help prevent power struggles later.

Let's commit to action rather than inaction. Let's help our children learn to control themselves while they're young when it can be learned.

Chapter 8 Application

1. What did you learn about authority in your childhood? Was it usually fair? Caring? Scary? Absent?

How did your a) father figure, and b) mother figure handle power and authority?

Did you ever dislike or resent their style?

Did you ever consciously try to be different than them? Could you disagree with authority when growing up and not be punished?

2. Do you feel comfortable with parental power?

Is there a hierarchy of influence in the family or is it a one person, one vote democracy?

If it is a hierarchy, how does a parent keep it from being a dictatorship?

3. On the continuum of active or passive, how would you rate your parenting style? Your mate's? What are the strengths and weaknesses for each style?

4. Do you use physical re-directive techniques with young children or do you tend to talk and reason while a child continues in the objectionable behavior?

5. Why is passivity not the same thing as giving into others? How can a Christian be sensitive and assertive?

6. Did you ever promise yourself you wouldn't be like one of your parent figures in a particular area? If yes, how does that affect you now? Could some of "them" still be inside "us"? Is there a downside to being compelled NOT to be like somebody?

Homeschooling for Life

Dr. Dale Simpson

Section 2: Marriage

Chapter 9: Marriage in a Paint Can

"All marriages are happy - it's the living together afterwards that causes all the trouble."

- Unknown

The smile quickly vanished from Tom's face.

You may have experience in putting a dent in your car, but few of us know how difficult it is to smooth that dent out to a flat surface. Repairing a fender and painting an automobile seem pretty straight forward at first thought. Sanding the surface, laying in fiberglass filler where needed, and sanding until it feels smooth usually ticks right along. But if you know anything about automobile body work, you know that the imperfections in the surface of the car jump out the moment you spray any primer paint onto it. Imperfections you were sure had been sanded smooth stand out like pimples on a prom night face the moment they are touched with paint. It is common to spray primer onto the surface so that the worker can see the blemishes and continue to shape the area.

Marriage, like auto body work, will illuminate things in yourself that you might not want on the front page of the local newspaper. It has made me face so much in myself that I didn't know was there or didn't want to see. Day to day living with the pressures of someone knowing you during the whole day and not just when you are on your best behavior causes you to confront all aspects of your personality. As one person put it, "It goes against one's constitution to be amiable to the same person day in and day out." It challenges you to be teachable and will reveal areas where you are not. In marriage, as in parenting, you will find yourself saying some of the things your parents said.

Strong emotion is like a violent snowstorm that makes it difficult for you to know where you are and find the path to reach your objective. It can be lethal and, over time, it can kill the connection and bonding in the marriage if not handled right. And just like that snow when it turns to ice on the ground, it can freeze you in place and because of your hurt and pride, simply render you emotionally immobile.

Companionship is what we need, and this is the ultimate objective for marriage. We need companionship and emotional intimacy to break our isolation and our aloneness. As in the story of Genesis when man had everything, including more pets than the law allows, God said that he was alone. We need another human being and not another pet. In an earthly sense, we need more than just talking to God. We need a relationship where we are knowing the other person and are being known at a profound level to fulfill this deep need. True emotional intimacy from another human being can be for us as important as oxygen.

Marriage, with its faithfulness and loyalty to another person, is an unspeakably profound experience. Commitment, which many people in this day and age are afraid of, is paralleled by nothing else in life. The converse, when the marital bond is broken by abandonment or infidelity, is staggeringly destructive.

Those of us who have not had to face marital unfaithfulness can count ourselves among the fortunate, and we should be deeply thankful. Those who have experienced brokenness can tell you the heartbreak that is involved. God acknowledges the depth of a broken relationship when He gives clear permission to divorce because of a break in this bond. Even though Scripture says that God hates divorce, an abandonment of one's commitment is so deep that it prompted Him to accommodate man by giving a writ of divorce.

As a psychologist I see couples who have weathered such a break, and now the offending party wants me to do something to get the other person to stay in the marriage. Many offending parties want to minimize the damage that such a break creates. Can you shatter a crystal vase and expect it to be glued quickly back together? As I have heard others in counseling over the years realize the importance of loyalty, it has greatly reinforced my personal commitment to morality in my marriage.

Another thing I have realized about marriage is that there are partial truths tossed around relating to marriage that are worth examining. One of them is that it's not so important who you marry, as who you are in marriage. I believe this is not the full picture. I agree that we all need to start with ourselves in marriage. It is critically important to know who we are and how we behave in marriage. Trying to change our mates or criticize them is not the road to marital happiness. Repeatedly, I see that I have a lifetime of things to work on in my marriage before I'll be able to say that I am a totally godly, healthy person.

Having said that, who you marry is absolutely critical. People who marry outside the faith, who marry others who have major emotional wounds or destructive habits, are in a different place than those who marry people without these characteristics.

This is not to say that some of those marriages cannot work or that God cannot do tremendous things in a relationship like that. But who you marry is a large part of the equation and it determines what you have to work with. Marrying someone who is of similar beliefs and is reasonably healthy emotionally, who knows how to love, and who has expectations of life in the same ball park as you means much to the marital union.

Many couples are thankful that they found someone with whom they were compatible. Over the years they see how much it helped them focus their energies on working out a few things rather than having to struggle for common interests and perspective on the world. It is a blessing to have similar views of life. Marriage has seasons in the lifecycle. Remaining married for many years will find you plowing through the midlife season, and with it comes particular issues that were not prominent at other times.

As you move to the later years, still other seasonal changes will occur and must be managed. Just as God has built in an unfolding in physical maturation, so He also has a social and emotional development that occurs across the span of life. A person learns that one can accept and plan for these changes or one can ignore or even try to fight them and put them off. We should seek ways to accept what God brings our way through the adventure of marriage and have the courage to submit each day to Him.

Another marriage myth (and a dangerous one at that) is that Christians get married only to give and not take. Women are especially prone to this error because being a help-mate can sound like they are to minister to their husbands without regard to their own needs.

Christian marriage entails two individuals becoming one. It involves ministry but it is much more than ministry. It demands great self-control, self-denial and giving. But it requires even more. It requires being a real person, someone who can "speak the truth in love," someone who will not purposely deny the other sexual fulfillment, someone who could confront you if you sin. Even the Proverbs 31 woman does not define herself completely by her husband. She is no passive person or she could never be a wise business woman or someone who can hire good servants.

A healthy Christian marriage requires two people who can be loving, giving, assertive, firm and real, "As iron sharpens iron, so one man (spouse?) sharpens another." (Prov. 27:17) You don't sharpen your spouse with tissue paper. The self-effacing, passive, "always giving" women are likely candidates for burn-out, depression, and health problems. Some of these people can last many years in the role of "I have no needs," but this martyr role is doomed to fail and it will fail to give the spouse and the children someone to help knock the rough edges off. I can tell you if my wife was just a "yes" person and not different from me, I would not have grown over the years in ways God wanted. Living in the community of a family stretches each person because of differences. There is no other way to experience marital growth except through the differences.

Working through hurt and emotional pain is a necessary part of the path to emotional intimacy. Just as suffering was part of God's eternal plan for the redemption of man, so working through the pain of our humanity and the hurts that can be experienced in a relationship helps accomplish the things of God. Of course, no one in his right mind would pray for pain or discomfort, and I don't see myself as a person particularly tolerant of loneliness or not getting my needs met. But there is much to learn in working through the maintenance of a loving relationship and I suspect far more of my lessons have been learned because of the healthy processing of pain than through the successes and the joys.

So, remember the lessons of the car body repairman. Let the process of your marriage illuminate the things you need to keep working on. Value and celebrate the ways a loyal, committed, assertive relationship files the rough spots off each other. Give the process to God as He shapes you into what He wants you to be.

Chapter 9 Application

1. What things have been revealed to you about yourself in marriage? What has been revealed in your spouse?

2. What improvements have you seen in yourself as a result of the stress of living together? What have you seen in your spouse?

3. Do you find it difficult to give in your marriage? Do you find it difficult to take in your marriage?

4. Do you and your partner value the differences in each other, even if they are frustrating at times? If not, are you willing to consciously seek to do this?

5. What differences in your spouse benefit you?

6. Have you decided that pain can be useful in your personal growth?

Chapter 10: Marriage Roles or Rules?

> *"An ideal wife is any woman who has an ideal husband."*
>
> — Unknown

Cindy came to the counseling session discouraged, defeated, guilt ridden, and depressed. "I've read this book and I've been to marriage retreats. I've tried to live up to the lives of certain Christian marriage authors and now found out they are divorcing. I still am so unfulfilled in my marriage. What does it really mean to be in a Christian marriage?"

A few generations ago when roles were socially prescribed in a rather monolithic way, people functioned with less anxiety. They may or may not have liked their roles, but there was much less struggle over the choices since there were few perceived choices to be made. Today, in a world filled with choices, it would be easy to find security in rigid, prescribed roles. With all that is written on Christian marriage and family life, I am careful to look for clear Scriptural statements when considering certain roles I read about. I don't want to add my own thinking to Scripture.

What we do know is that husbands are commanded to love their wives as Christ loved the church and gave Himself for her. Wives are told to adapt and submit themselves to their husbands. We also know that the husband, in only one place in Scripture, is described as the head of the wife "as Christ is head of the church." What could this headship statement mean? And why doesn't

Scripture go into detail about specifics of the roles of husband and wife (e.g. men manage the money, repair the home, buy the car, make decisions about what the family does, etc.)? Surely the principles of teamwork and mutual respect are more important to Him than specifics of who writes the checks. Those cultural and preferential differences may not be as important as the godly way a couple relates.

It is interesting to read books or hear seminars focused upon the biblical roles of men and women. Many things said are good and deal with the broad principles expressed in God's Word. Some writers share practical and specific suggestions — things they have found helpful in their marriage or family. But some speakers and writers in conservative Christian circles fill in the blanks with their own specifics without qualifying it with "this is just my way and not thus saith the Lord." This is part of the "adding to Scripture" problem. I've even heard a pastor and educator say that he is the one in charge of breast feeding his children... he just lets his wife help him. This, I believe, is preposterous and designed to help a man feel in control but has nothing to do with either what Scripture says or what is even reasonable.

Of course, we need structure — some fleshing out of the principles that direct us. When you look at the whole Bible, I think you will find some broader principles that should guide whatever specifics a couple applies in their home. Here are some of the principles spoken of in the Bible which I think can be found in godly marriages.

Teamwork and mutual responsibility for the marriage and home characterize godly couples. Teamwork seems to involve, among other things, the willingness to listen to, consult with, and communicate to one another. If one person seems overly dominant or overly responsible for marital or family life, it is difficult to maintain pleasant emotions and true closeness or love.

Some women seem to carry the whole burden for maintaining the marriage and family and this is too lopsided to be the way a family should function. Spreading the load across more than one person is like spreading your weight with snow-shoes so that you can stay above the soft snow and not fall through. When stress hammers us, the marriages that are held up by two tend to keep their heads above the snowline.

Mutual respect has to be another characteristic found in healthy and fulfilling marriages. The consistent communication that the other partner's feelings are equally important strengthens the marital bond. In fact, we should strive to consider our partner first in order to combat our inherent narcissism. Many marriages I know of would be revolutionized if they could just communicate that they see each other as co-heirs. Ask yourself how long you would last in a job where you felt disrespected by your colleagues or boss. I doubt we would consider that place to be a reasonable environment to hang our hat. So it is with the marriage relationship.

A third trait in Christian marriage is a demonstration of sacrifice and mutual giving. Surely marriage is to be give and take. Too often the ability to sacrifice (in everything from getting up with a sick child to compromising toward a spouse's decision) is not held in high esteem. If partners will view sacrificing as a way to develop themselves, they will grow without feeling cheated. If the giving in a marriage is one-sided, chronic problems will emerge.

Some degree of humility and teachability characterizes the Christian marriage. This is closely related to mutual
respect and should grow as we learn more about each other and life. Unfortunately, defensiveness, fear of criticism and failure, and poorly communicating our frustration keep many couples from knowing how to learn from each other. The Scriptural principle couldn't be any clearer: wise people are teachable, fools

are not. The secondary principle is that a wise person will make what he has to share digestible and not just throw it out insensitively. Good marriage partners know how to talk about problems respectfully and learn from each other.

Companions should be willing to seek the good. Couples who work toward a solution rather than abandoning the process of love show true spirituality. Relationships really do mean the most in the Christian home because they mean the most to God. A heart that can get past its hurt and anger and move toward honest reconciliation is a heart worth knowing. This may take time and much struggle, but the Christian heart seeks any healthy, respectful way to resolve relational damage.

You may want to use this chapter as a stimulus for a "state of the union" discussion with your spouse. Review what each of you thinks of your roles and the principles discussed here. Share lovingly and honestly where your heart is.

Always be discerning when you are asked to move past principles in Scripture to specifics. They may be good suggestions. They may be what you want to build into your marriage. But be careful about using ways that work for you to dictate how all marriages should be. Remember, adding to Scripture can be just as much of a problem as taking away from Scripture.

Chapter 10 Application

1. Discuss with your spouse the roles you saw in your parents' marriages. What have you kept in your marriage? What have you changed?

2. Are roles and responsibilities clear in your marriage?

3. What role and expectations would you like to see different in your marriage? Can you express them to your mate?

4. If you are a Christian, what does the Bible say are clear roles in all cultures? Find the passages and read them for a clear understanding.

5. Who gives more in your marriage, you or your spouse? Why do you think this is so? Are you satisfied with that? There are times when giving without demanding anything in return is best. When is it best in your marriage?

Dr. Dale Simpson

Chapter 11: Your Best Retirement Plan

"A successful marriage requires falling in love many times, always with the same person."

- Mignon McLaughlin

Moments before the big blowout

Kids love to see their mom and dad hold hands. They will often react with "Yuck," but inside, they enjoy the feeling of knowing their parents are bonded and together in their lives. The security in children brought about by a secure marriage is hard to overestimate. Appropriate tenderness and affection shown between marriage partners in front of the children also helps model healthy expressions of love and companionship.

Your marriage began before children came along. It will be there after they leave. Your marriage is your best retirement plan. It is, in a way, the start and finish of the family life cycle. Nothing, save our relationship to God, can be more important to the family and to the process of rearing children. This companionship and social connectedness is fundamental to happiness (see Chapter 8). We are social creatures, and we must know and be known in a human relationship in order to be at peace. This startling fact is illustrated in Genesis 2:18 when, after creating the worlds, the ecosystem on earth, and Adam, God says a most amazing thing-- and He says this after walking and talking with Adam in the pre-fall garden. God says, "It is not good that you are alone." How many Christians would tell someone, "You're never alone with God?" How many of us would say "If you have no one in your life, just talk with God, and He will be all you need"?

Well, God Himself said that in the human condition, just simply communing with God does not break social isolation. What was God's solution? He made another human (Eve), someone like Adam yet different than him. This was God's solution to the "aloneness" Adam was experiencing before the Fall and even while he related to God.

Of course, I am not trying to draw any crazy theological conclusions from this. Yet consider that this emotional intimacy between two human beings appears to be necessary for fulfillment. Yes, God is the one who meets our needs. But He does it through earthly means such as food, shelter, water, and people. It is critical that we get much of our needs for social connectedness met through our marriages. As we have our needs met, we can then be better equipped to do the demanding jobs of parenting and homeschooling our children. As we meet needs within the marriage, we are strengthening relational skills that we will continue to need long after the children leave home.

A young marriage can suffer significant loss in its ability to experience quality time. This loss often occurs as children are added, particularly with budding careers and new family adjustments also in the picture. Closeness within the marriage doesn't necessarily grind to a halt, but it does tend to drift and get supplanted by such demands as children, sleep, and making a living. The excitement of early relationship and newfound companionship can dwindle as a routine settles into the family. A man typically is pursuing school or a job, and full-time moms are giving themselves to the care of the children and organizing home life. Other demanding scenarios find both spouses pursuing careers at breakneck speed, sometimes with unexpected pregnancies occurring. Critical maintenance tasks in the marriage are often subordinated to the other necessities.

Family stress from any source can make it harder for couples to take the time to do the necessary things to keep the marriage healthy. When people are over-taxed mentally or physically, they often want to do something with low demands and a high "pamper" factor. Watching television or going to movies can become more attractive options as stress levels increase. Activities that carry any measure of responsibility can feel taxing and burdensome. Even going out to dinner can seem less attractive than simply sitting at home.

Men often are slower to react to emotional needs and are less likely to initiate quality interpersonal time, in favor of more production-oriented behaviors. They are likely to be the last to recognize necessary companionship needs. Rather, they attend to them only when they become almost impossible to ignore

Think about the people who have affected your marriage. Your parents, parental figures, even grandparents play a part in your memories of what marriages are, and in what skills and patterns you bring to your role. Your spouse is equally impacted by his or her family and the legacies left behind. These effects can be positive and enhancing, or they can make stable emotional intimacy difficult to maintain. They can even be negative motivators (e.g. "I'll never do what my parents did,") though often we have internalized more of their behavior than we care to admit.

Chapter 11 Application

1. Take 20-30 minutes to look through photo albums with your mate, recalling as much as possible about key pictures from their growing up. Play psychologist…find out what makes that person tick. Alternate next week to your photos and remember your early years.

2. Discuss with your spouse what your parents' marriages are or were like. What were the good things and what do you not want to repeat?

3. Discuss together what you like about each other. Explain two or three things you wish you could change to be a better mate. Tell your mate one thing he or she could do that would improve your closeness.

4. Head to the nearest go-cart track. Race your spouse around the track.

5. Have a squirt gun fight in the back yard. Men, let the women have use of the Super Soaker.

6. Go out to a nice restaurant after dinner and order something small, like pie and coffee. Talk about anything but children and work.

7. Look over your wedding pictures together. On another night, let the kids look with you while you comment.

8. Develop the habit of taking a minimum of 10 minutes each evening (after the children are in bed) discussing how each other's day went and what was important. Thirty minutes or more is not uncommon in good marriages.

9. Shut off the TV. Eliminate most of your television screen time including the news for a week. I also recommend getting news and current events primarily from printed sources rather than video sources.

You may have other enjoyable and enriching activities to enliven your marriage. Commit to doing at least one thing each week or two. Don't take your marriage for granted.

Homeschooling for Life

Dr. Dale Simpson

Section 3: Family

Chapter 12: For Dads Only

"What a father says to his children is not heard by the world, but it will be heard by posterity."

- Unknown

I want to share something I heard recently about wisdom. Somebody was asked, "How did you get to be so wise?" The reply was, "Well, it wasn't that hard. I have good judgment, and good judgment comes from experience, and experience, well, that comes from having bad judgment." Isn't that true? We don't learn as much by success as we do by failure. Malcom Muggeridge said in all his life he never learned anything important except through pain. If we pay attention and let our failures teach us, and if we aren't too defensive, we're going to gather wisdom as we travel along this journey of life. If not, we'll repeat the same mistakes. None of us have all the answers.

We need to use our failures and our mistakes in a way that will produce wisdom so we'll be better equipped as men in the different roles we perform. The most important role we'll play is likely our role as father.

There are many models in the world today of what men are supposed to be and do. Many speakers and authors have given you their perspectives on this. My perspective may be different from theirs, and yours may be different from mine, and that's fine. I am not God; I don't tell people how to act. Even the Bible does not necessarily nail down who in the home writes the checks, buys the car, etc. It gives us principles. From a Christian perspective there's a lot of flexibility. God didn't spell it out in detail or in such rigid roles that we can't be flexible according to our situation and culture.

One thing I want to emphasize is that men terribly underestimate how important they are to the emotional life of the family. Whether you're good at emotional or relational things or not, whatever you do is critical. You affect people in tremendous ways. Your kids are internalizing you and your wife. Children are becoming your reaction to them whether you like it or not. You are interacting with them. That's why it's wise to be together, to encourage each other, to strengthen each other, to help each other when we mess up. Building personalities in our children is really one of the most important things we can do with our lives. Whatever you do, don't underestimate your value interpersonally with your family.

Where do we learn our role model for fathering? We start with our own father, or stepfather, or some father figure in our life. Maybe some of us were raised without a man in the home, so we're still looking for a father figure. We are also influenced by the role models in the media and our tendency to model after observed behavior.

Some of the modern-day role models have to do with successful positions in the business or sports world such as head football coaches. I heard a popular NFL coach, say, "The life of an NFL coach consists of going to work at six in the morning, getting home about eleven at night, and doing that seven days a week all year long. You know, after a while, that can lead to burnout." This man is one of our role models, a successful football coach, a man who gets accolades, who wins Superbowls. This driven behavior isn't smart. Granted, it's hard work. The successful coach is a hard worker. These actions can win Superbowl rings, but they can't win a wife's heart. These men can't be a good father to their children. These kinds of men will be lucky if they become nice grandfathers to their grandchildren. These driven men will not likely succeed with their children in the way they succeed in sports.

So, there are trade-offs. When you're saying "yes" to something, you're saying "no" to something else. Let me tell you the "no" that hurts the most. Saying "no" to quality time with your children will cause them to learn to live without you. They'll sometimes develop behavioral symptoms and they'll live without you. You have to choose between being there for your child or being with the career trade-off in your life. The driven career man isn't a healthy role model. I don't even consider it truly successful. If I'm on my deathbed looking back at my life and I'm one of the top fifty psychologists in the country, but I don't know my children and I don't have a close relationship with my wife, I'll consider myself an utter failure in life. Saint Paul saw the same thing when he said one mark of a Christian leader is to have his home life in order. (I Cor:13 – "If I do not have love, I am nothing!")

It's also tremendously important for our wives and our children to have security based in love, where they know we aren't loving them because they're acting right and then removing affection when they're acting wrong. Men frequently exhibit this contingency. When our kids mess up, the consequences should not be the withdrawal of our affection and love. This is emotionally deadly. We need to show them affirmation, cherish them, accept them — "the good, the bad, and the ugly" in them. There isn't anything they can do that's too big for us to handle with them, even when they are angry with us. Can you let your kids be mad at you in a respectful way? Are you big enough and secure enough to accept your children's anger, especially when it is aimed at you?

The generation who raised me in the 50's and early 60's considered it disrespectful when you became angry at a parent. Just feeling anger was disrespectful. You were never taught to be angry in a healthy, godly way. You were just told, "Don't do that!" Did that make the anger go away? No, we just went to our rooms, turned up the radio as loud as we could, and invented the 1960's. We, in part, were saying, "Somebody listen to me!"

Be sure you're big enough to let your children feel fear, joy, anger, or hurt in your relationship to them because they're going to feel it, whether you want them to or not. The difference will be that if you can handle those feelings, they will be more able to handle them and figure out a healthy way to express those feelings. If you show you can't handle unpleasant feelings, they get pushed down within the child, reemerging as some malady or symptom later.

If a son can come angrily to you and say, "Dad, I'm really mad at you because you won't let me go bowling…I'm mad at you because you told me you'd fix my bike and you didn't do it… I'm mad at you because you yelled at me," it is a healthy sign. In our family this is considered respectful because he is telling me about feelings he had and giving me honest information, i.e. "speaking the truth in love" (Eph 4:15). Now, if he slams a door in your face, if he says you're stupid, that's disrespectful. The anger isn't the problem, but how it is expressed.

If I train him that it's okay to react disrespectfully in anger, he won't stay on a job very long, nor will he stay in a marriage. Proper anger expression is a necessary skill in life. If we fail to teach truly proper outlets for anger, life will be needlessly difficult.

As a father, I want to help you in your role as fathers or father figures to come to terms with your feelings and to route them in a respectful, healthy way so that this learning process can be reflected in your children. Yet in conflict, many of us get really defensive and angry. We shout and send kids to their rooms. We aren't able to say, "Honey, I know you're angry with me, but you're shouting, and that's disrespectful. You need to get control because if you don't, I'm going to discipline you because I love you. I know you're mad at me and you need to look at your choices right now." We have to help them learn to express themselves.

Let me tell you a secret about anger. Underneath anger there's something deeper. Anger is a defense mechanism. It's a secondary emotion. When you're angry, ask yourself these questions: What am I hurting about? In what am I disappointed? What am I feeling rejected about? What am I sad about? Some form of hurt, loss, helplessness or not getting your way, is always underneath anger. We're looking for the source—be it hurt or fear or a blocked objective. That's the key to control.

Anger is okay to talk about, but the thing we want to strive for is talking about the hurt underneath. This hurt is even more intimate, deeper, more on-target, and it will more easily address the underlying problem.

Look for the source. Look for the pain or hurt underneath. Talk to your children about it. That's dealing with the inner life. That's where we need to deal with our family. We don't want to stay on the surface all the time. I have a plaque in my office that says, "Better than being the head of the family is being the heart of it." Let's be the heart of our family. That's where everybody really lives. That's where eternity is.

Chapter 12 Application

1. How do you contribute to your family besides providing an income, mowing the lawn, or changing the oil in the car?

2. View your possessions as a format for teaching your child. For example, can you see a $20 tool that was ruined by the rain, as an instrument for teaching your child responsibility and consequences?

3. When you are on your death bed, who do you want by your side? Why do you want them to be there? What do you want them to remember about you? What do you need to do to make the end come out like you want?

4. Love and caring can be expressed with a hug, a few words of praise, or a few minutes of listening. Pick one simple thing a day to express caring to each child and your wife.

5. Are you a strong enough man to accept your child's feelings and thoughts even if they are different from yours? Do you think that accepting feelings is the same as tolerating misbehavior?

Chapter 13: What to Do with Emotions

"Let me embrace thee, sour adversity.
For wise men will say it is the wisest course."

- Shakespeare

Let's face it. We have something within us that can take us from the heights of unspeakable joy to the depths of despair. It can produce rage and cowering terror. This "it" is our set of emotions and the limbic system in our brain that drives the process. Emotions are our companions throughout life.

Some people seem to express every whim of emotion in magnified ways. Others seem to be so stoic, you wonder if they feel at all. But unlike Mr. Spock on Star Trek, full-blooded humans are not always controlled by reason. Even people who keep their emotions hidden have them. Emotions enrich life, their color helping define what it is to be human. They are useful and can produce great art, music, or a love poem. We worship God with them, too.

Feelings can also be problematic. They can be scary; scary because they sometimes push us to do horrible, insensitive things to others. Often, it feels better to give in to them and ignore the consequences. Feelings can also feel so delicious that they override our judgment as we give in to them.

The homeschooling family, like other families, has the full range of feelings woven through the fabric of its experience. It is clear that we must deal, with our emotions. But what does it mean to deal with feelings? How do we teach our children to deal with emotions?

First, feelings can go underground if not identified and consciously managed. Simply ignoring and hiding feelings does not deal with them adequately. Too often this repression leads to growing resentment, frustration, discouragement, and depression. What appears to be handling emotions is in reality the denial of emotions. This occurs most frequently in families where parents are uncomfortable with their own emotions and must negate any expression of unpleasant feelings from the child. Fear or shame are frequently used to control and suppress feelings. These techniques are quite powerful and yet quite damaging.

Second, stoicism is not the healthy or Christian way of approaching emotions. The refusal to accept emotions as important and valid aspects of our humanity contradicts how we are made. It denies any meaning to suffering and makes unimportant any feelings involved in relationships. We know the Bible shows real men and women with real feelings. Feelings are also shown in the life of Jesus and are attributed to the Godhead.

Thirdly, what we can identify within ourselves we can most likely control. What we don't properly label and catch will control us. The flip side of this is expressed often in Alcoholics Anonymous circles: "We are as sick as our secrets." To develop and maintain self- control, we must be skilled at identifying feelings and managing them effectively. Emotions are a signal. They give us valuable information. We would be foolish to ignore them simply because at times the information is not flattering. For example, knowing the difference between sadness and jealousy is extremely important in self-management. Yet, so many people are incapable of distinguishing the two within themselves. Helping our children correctly label their inner life is at least as important as helping them dissect the parts of a sentence.

Fourth, we can't help but teach our children about emotions. We do it implicitly (how they see us handle feelings; how we respond to them) or explicitly (the direct statements about emotions and relationships we make to them). Children will see the style of handling anger and hurt that each of their parents has learned. Each child, to varying degrees, will internalize some of these styles along with the "rules" of emotions taught by the family.

If handling feelings involves the process of accurately identifying emotions, the reasons for the emotions, and making healthy, godly choices in the face of those emotions, then how do we teach this?

1. Resolve to be an excellent teacher of emotional skills as well as academic skills.

2. Identify your style of handling pleasant and unpleasant feelings.

3. Resolve that it is acceptable for your children to feel (not do) anything. A certain emotion may or may not be desirable and may even tempt us to do evil — but if one feels it, it exists and can be named, accepted and dealt with as real.

4. Reflect to children the central emotion you hear before questioning or instructing them. For example, "You sound angry…do you know what you are mad about?" This reflecting of the feeling accomplishes a number of important tasks. It "joins" the child so he feels heard, valued, and understood, not alone. It also provides a label to connect with a particular feeling, educating the child to what is happening inside him.

Finally, it prevents us from saying something inappropriate or discrediting his feelings.

5. Express feelings using the format: "I feel" (emotion) "when or because..." Example: "I feel hurt when you shout at me." Do not use blame or threaten. Simply report feelings.

6. Encourage kids to express feelings. Help them learn to manage anger at authority figures rather than to deny it. Teach them that the phrase "I feel angry with you, Daddy, because..." is not disrespect but healthy, godly expression. Teach them that disrespectful behavior (i.e. saying. "you're stupid") will be disciplined, (but that hurt and anger are not bad to express in healthy ways).

7. Never discipline or punish your child for having feelings. If misbehavior occurs when they are expressed, address the behavior with discipline and not the emotion. Teach your child that there are healthy ways to express the emotions he feels.

Are feelings friends or enemies? They seem to be important facts about our inner life that give us valuable information and create motivation for behavior. Emotions can, if left unchecked, cause great damage and for this reason they must be controlled if we are to have successful relationships. The interesting paradox is that if we face them and experience them, we have a chance to control them. If we try to ignore them, they will go underground where they will ooze out in some form that is less controllable. Like bad news from a physician, we need to pay attention because there may be things we can do to effect a cure. If we refuse to hear troubling news, we will be at the mercy of the problem.

Acknowledging and accepting your child's feelings are ways to express God's love to him. It is the kind of acceptance from the heart of God that we experience regarding our feelings. God helps us face our emotions honestly, and He guides us to healthy solutions. Be sure to educate your kids with regard to their emotions.

Forgiveness: A Matter of the Heart

You know, it's easy to say, "I'm sorry," "I'm sorry your dog died," or "I'm sorry if you misunderstood me." Most people can be sorry for things. Most people find it easy to wish bad things wouldn't have happened.

But there are words that hang in the throat; phrases that evaporate near the lips; hard words tied to the heart, words that express humility and responsibility. In our families, these are usually the best words.

In all long-term relationships, pain and anger surface. Even in our relationship to God, pain and anger can occur in us. As parents, one of our jobs is to educate children regarding the management of pain and anger in relationships. We do this first through example or modeling. It's always the Christian's first level of teaching others. Second, we give them instructions and practice with methods of resolving hurts and wrongs.

A favorite method of mine is a three-part forgiveness model that incorporates the best in healthy and godly behavior. It is a useful guide ensuring that the wrong has been dealt with and not just covered over. So many times in the Christian community we push children into a pseudo-forgiveness that amounts to denial rather than facing the truth. We minimize feelings and the relational consequences of the wrong by too quickly telling people to forgive and forget. The result is often a family's wrongs are never redemptive or remedial, but rather are incomplete, hindering real change. It reflects our own discomfort with tension and often enables chronic misbehavior to continue.

Let's look at an example. Sally is building a tower with wooden blocks. Her brother, Tim, runs by and pushes her building down with a crash. Sally gets angry and yells at Tim. Mom walks in and after she understands the series of events, says, "Tim, tell Sally you are sorry."

Tim answers, almost under his breath, "Sorry."

"Now there is no reason for you to be angry, Sally. Just build your tower again," Mom says as she walks away. Does this apology adequately deal with the situation?

The next time you offend your spouse or children, try this method if you aren't doing something similar. First, confess the wrong behavior in a simple sentence without any "buts" or blames. (e.g. "I was wrong to yell at you — you do not deserve this.") Second, repent of your behavior by committing to change. (e.g. "I am committed to changing this with you," or, "I need to handle my anger in a better way.") Third, ask for forgiveness. (e.g. "Would you forgive me?") This humbly accepts responsibility for the relational consequences and asks for the other person to face his choice of how to deal with the offense.

Forgiveness, someone once said, is costly remembering. It is a choice to give up something. It is action in the face of pain and only has virtue because of the reality of the wrong. By directly asking forgiveness, we show what process is really going on...making right an offense.

Forgiveness is then seen to be more than regret. It is the punctuation at the end of a sentence. Forgiveness completes the emotional work that is necessary for reconciliation. Being sorry only describes an inner state but does not call for any particular action. Simple regret often avoids the humility called for in true repentance. Acknowledging regret is certainly better than silence or blame. But a family atmosphere with only "I'm sorry's" and pseudo-forgiveness that denies the pain leads to little genuine change. Families who walk through an honest experience of pain, expression, and forgiveness will produce real conviction in their members.

Asking for forgiveness is a strength. Facing the pain of interpersonal sins, and not glossing over it is of God. Take a moment to review your family's health regarding forgiveness. Be sure you practice real forgiveness that properly acknowledges the wrong and its impact. Confess to your family an interpersonal wrong you may have committed toward them this week. Teaching this relationship skill gives them something not found in a book…the experience of true reconciliation.

Chapter 13 Application

1. Why is forgiveness different than denial or ignorance?

2. Have you recently asked your mate or child to forgive you? If so, how did you feel?

3. What does a person feel and think if a loved one wrongs him but never takes responsibility for it? What if someone makes excuses for his bad behavior?

4. If someone is upset with you, does that mean you did something wrong and need to ask for forgiveness? Why or why not?

5. Have you been asked to forgive an authority figure in your life after they wronged you? If so, how did you feel? What did it do to the relationship?

6. Are feelings really okay? Can you think of unpleasant emotions as useful rather than wrong?

7. What emotions do you have the hardest time managing?

8. What emotions do you have the hardest time feeling or expressing?

9. Are emotions a part of our relationship to each other and to God?

10. If we cannot deal with certain emotions, how will that affect our children?

Dr. Dale Simpson

Chapter 14: The Time Management Blues

"All my possessions for a moment of time"

- Queen Elizabeth I

A really dumb question

I hate time. It always seems to embarrass and dominate me. My track record in taming it is not so great. You'd think after years of living within its domain, I would be better at anticipating and managing time. Repeatedly, I'm late, without the moments needed to complete something. I'm often late with clinical reports at work. And my editors know to take my stated deadlines with large doses of skepticism.

Other adults seem to be equally inept at living with time constraints. I've noticed that our child's first soccer game of the season is always scheduled so that pictures must be taken prior to each game. Team and individual pictures at every 15-minute intervals followed by games at preset times is like lining up dominoes close together for hours and hoping they don't fall. The day drags on as adults try to make up for lost time and, like Congress trying to balance the budget, they become more indebted to it. A visiting alien would conclude that adult humans are not very intelligent creatures in their management of time.

Rick was a friend who seemed to know how to harness and dominate time. I would marvel at his detailed and disciplined attention to even small blocks of time. He didn't have children, but he was married and seemed to relate reasonably well to others. Working beside Rick was like watching a magician perform a mystifying trick. I just couldn't figure out how he did it. But guys like Rick can seem so rigid. I get discouraged about ever making their style work for me.

The Christian community is also affected by the world's emphasis on activity and success. I know of too many missionaries who sent their child away to boarding school so they could carry on the work of ministry. One large Christian organization refuses to let workers home school because it takes away from the work. What does this communicate about the importance of family or children?

Ever since the assembly line was invented, we've stressed productivity over the quality of the job. Pleasure in the activity of work was the least concern for Henry Ford. Enjoying the journey and craftsmanship of one's labor became lost in the drive to produce more. Rather than using time for an end, we became driven by time for someone else's purposes. We live in a hurried world. How many times are we saying to children, "Hurry up... we're late"? If we are poor managers of time, they will likely be that way. But managing time well is not necessarily having every moment of the day filled with activities. Scheduling should serve us, not the other way around, bringing about the balance that God intends.

In the past, families were not as fragmented as in modern life with each person going off to separate daily routines. Families worked together in proximity to each other. Daily life was shared and each person's experience was related. Fathers were an integral part of daily life before the Industrial Revolution took us away from the home. Now men are often irrelevant in the daily life at home. We usually cannot interact with our spouse or children when working. We must choose one or the other. Even in the homeschooling family where much of daily life is shared, the father's daily work life is usually removed from the home. This constant demand to choose concerns me, not because I can't make decisions, but because there are no clear cut, legalistic rules that would comfort me. C.S. Lewis once made the point that we are forever at odds with time because we were made for eternity. Like aliens, we languish in an environment we don't understand.

I struggle with what my lifestyle teaches our children about time and its management. What does God want me to do with it? The challenge of how to work hard and give a fair day's work for a fair wage (a biblical principle) and also to be a good steward of my emotional and physical life with regular relaxation and recuperative pleasures is a formidable one. Where is the balance between the necessity of working and importance of relationships? Keeping this balance in the busyness of life is like trying to juggle bubbles in a hurricane. I confess my failure in this area, and I feel uncomfortable exhorting others when my life needs addressing.

Nevertheless, time is not a complete enemy. Time gives limits and helps provide meaning. It structures our lives so that what we choose to do means something. If we had limitless time, we could always put off until tomorrow what we need to do today. Each person makes choices about what to do with his time, and these choices declare what is meaningful to that person. Think of it. The matters we attend to in our lives express what we value and for what we are living.

I'm learning how to delegate more responsibilities. I'm learning to spend money to pay for certain time-consuming things that would take me away from relationship time. I'm trying to pay attention to the details in the lives of my children just as I attend to details in other tasks. I'm hugging them more and looking into their eyes more. If I must set a time to have a project done, I'll double or triple my estimate of what it will take as a cushion to my poor judgment. Overall, I'm re-doubling my efforts to see each moment as God sees it and not as productivity experts see it. Time makes us all prisoners, but while in my jail cell, I'll at least be better organized and focus on the right uses of my time.

I pray the future will be different in my appreciation for the management of time. May we express God's values through our activities. May it not just be a flurry of words that are not acted upon. As the musician Bob Bennett says, "May the words of my mouth fall to my heart." Work hard. Play hard. Relate hard. Rest hard. Let's use our time wisely.

Chapter 14 Application

1. What does "performance oriented" mean to you? How do you want your family relationships described by the members of your family?

2. Do you feel overwhelmed by the demands on your time? Talk to your spouse about this. Are there important things you are not getting to? Why?

3. God is our Father. How do you communicate God's character and values to your family? Be specific.

Dr. Dale Simpson

Chapter 15: Self-Esteem - Is It Selfishness?

"Do not think more highly than you ought but think soberly..."

- St. Paul, Romans 12:3

"I worked harder than all of them..."

- St. Paul, 1 Cor. 15: 10; 2 Cor. 11:23

"Accept one another, then, just as Christ accepted you..."

- St. Paul, Romans 15:7

Since the 1970's, self-esteem has been a buzzword in schools and child care. Countless books extol the virtue and necessity of loving yourself and seeing good instead of bad inside. Quite rightly, Christians have scrutinized these writings and the philosophies underlying them. Over the years, I have read Christian material that ranges from whole-hearted endorsement of the self- esteem concept to vilifying it as the personification of humanistic evil. What is this self-esteem anyway?

Self-esteem is the emotional reaction we have to ourselves; our disposition to whom we are. This emotional evaluation of ourselves occurs in all humans and is similar to the way we form impressions of others. Humans appear to constantly assess things, people, and experiences that flow in and out of life. It is natural, then, that as we grow up, we come to some judgment about the goodness and badness of ourselves.

What contributes to this evaluation of the self? From shortly after birth (and to some degree even pre-birth), we are drawn to things that are pleasurable and satisfying. Likewise, we are distressed by, and want relief from, those things that are painful or uncomfortable. If the environment and the adults in our world provide relief and protection from distress in a reasonable amount of time, the world feels safe and trust begins. The infant, with no ability to distinguish self from the environment, concludes that he individually is good. With inconsistent or traumatic early experiences, the child concludes that he is bad or mostly bad. As children grow, they also internalize others' reactions to them, further contributing to a particular disposition toward the self.

This internalization, or taking in the attitude others have of the child, always happens. This developmental process is part of God's created program and cannot be prevented. Our only choice is what to have children internalize. This reality is staggering for the parent because we can see beyond the momentary pain visible in a child's eyes to the deeper, longer lasting damage we may create.

Self-esteem also grows from a budding sense of accomplishment and competence in this world. This child begins seeing himself succeed in conquering many of the things other people are conquering, causing him to feel a sense of personal effectiveness and equality with others. This is a natural stage of development that must be achieved to produce a mature person.

Self-esteem is not conceit or pride. Pride is an inadequate attempt to hide from or compensate for weakness and pain. Proud behavior is insecurity based, where the person is driven to convince others (in reality, to convince himself) that he is okay. When you see someone with a style of criticizing others and showing how he always does things better, you are seeing some of the outward manifestations of low self-esteem. Low self-esteem is also seen in overly aggressive and competitive people who are driven to win in everything. Many fathers are still acting out this insecurity by a compulsion to win at board games or basketball games they play with their children. Some men leave their children crying when they play checkers or wrestle on the floor all because of their must-win competitiveness and the fear of facing the feelings of inadequacy in themselves.

Low self-esteem can also be seen in depressive and passive behavior styles. Fear of failure and displeasing others can drive someone to adopt a please-at-all-cost approach to relationships. This results in a person with a fuzzy identity who cannot take a strong stand in relationships because of his dependency needs (the need to be reassured by others). These individuals can hide low self-esteem by trying to achieve perfect behavior. They can be over controlled and terribly afraid inside. How many of us were (or knew of someone who was) the child who acted "just right" and yet felt empty inside?

Low self-esteem creates a need for the person, whether he is compensating by aggressiveness or passivity, to prove something about the self...that it is good, smart, likable, better than others, competent...instead of worse than other people. Feeling more unworthy than other people... (that sinking feeling that can exist from childhood) must be handled somehow in order to make it through life.

As Christians, we know that corporately and individually we are morally bankrupt. We cannot erase the effects of our rebellious nature from the universe. We know that our faith is the only grace-based religion in the world. In that, we find freedom. Even as sinners, we are (albeit fallen) created in the image of God and we know that Christ died for us. Morally, as Christians, we know that all people are capable of the same set of rebellious, selfish attitudes and behaviors. There are no good and bad people from that point of view. There is level ground at the foot of the cross.

Yet we must not fall into "worm theology" that confuses our moral condition with our value as a person. To become preoccupied with our children's sinful nature and to see them only as selfish creatures who naturally don't want to learn is to miss the point and hold an extra-biblical position. This mistake is made more easily when one does not have a biblically-based perspective on development.

To be healthy in this world, our children do not need to feel like they are less than other people. They need to see we value them and internalize a godly emotional reaction to themselves. They need to feel what we fee as Christians, that they are "acceptable in the Beloved." They need to believe this so in moments where they do not feel it, they know they have other options. There are countless ways we can communicate value to our children. Here are just a few.

1. Choose to value them and their feelings. Make it a practice to look deep into their eyes and think of the tender, vulnerable person in there who is naturally seeking to learn who they are from you.

2. Communicate respect to them by asking them rather than ordering them to do things. It's still an implied order but it feels so much different to be asked. Also say "thank you" after they complete the task.

3. Face the effects of our emotional blow-ups. Since our children internalize what they think is our attitude toward them, make it a top priority to change if you are explosive. Pray, look into what

causes your behavior, and commit to your family that you will change it. Tell your children that they are not at fault when you blow up.

4. Regularly tell each child that you are "pleased"" and "satisfied" with them as a son or daughter. Do this when they haven't performed anything special. Do this ten minutes after you have had to discipline the child. Tell them regularly that they are just the way a child their age should be. Tell each child at various times that you would love to have five more just like them.

5. Help them feel competent in the things of life. Avoid over protection, which unwittingly strips away a sense of competence. Point out even embryonic success in a child's behavior. Teach them to fail with grace and dignity, not with shame and blame.

Self-esteem is an important factor in our children's development and in their ability to learn. We will leave inside each of our children a legacy of emotion that will define how they feel about themselves. Leave a good and godly work within them. Help them not fall in love with themselves (the Bible never directs us to be self-centered), but rather teach them to fall into acceptance of themselves. It's a wonderful gift we can give them.

Chapter 15 Application

1. Discuss the messages sent to you through the words and behavior of your parent figures. How do you think you handled these messages and the feelings you had?

2. What was your role in the family growing up? Were you the eldest? The eldest daughter? The baby? The only child? Daddy's helper? Little Mommy? The secret keeper? The clumsy underachiever? How much of that role do you play as an adult?

3. When are you hardest on yourself? Is the theme one of healthy regret and sadness or one of shame and internal abuse? What do you do when you feel this badly about yourself? Do you connect to someone or keep yourself isolated? What difference would this make?

4. Can you really abandon yourself to the reality of grace and accept God's love in spite of your behavior and heart? Does this view of grace help draw you to God even more?

5. How do you communicate your love to your children in a way that makes it unconditional? Do your spouse and children feel the security of your love leave when they do something wrong?

6. Consider having a family meeting and ask the children for ways you can be a better parent. Ask them specifically how they feel when you get mad and how you could make those times better.

7. What successes or accomplishments have helped you feel competent in the world? Think of your spouse and each child, asking, "In what things do they feel competent?" How can you help them feel competent?

Dr. Dale Simpson

Chapter 16: Why Won't You Just Say Something?

> *"He had all the qualities of a fireplace poker except its occasional warmth."*
>
> - Unknown

Joe and Mary came to my office with one main concern in their relationship. "We just don't communicate," said Mary.

As our session continued, I found out that their marriage had been filled with arguments followed by days without speaking to each other.

At the end of the first session, I told them that they clearly <u>did</u> communicate with each other. Their new mission was to learn to communicate <u>well</u> with each other.

Relationships make up our life, and to have a productive life, we must be equipped with relationship skills. Let's look at things that keep us from initiating communication with others. These are problems of omission rather than commission.

Inability to Identify the Inner Life

For many people, identifying their feelings and developing relationships is difficult or sometimes even impossible. Their awareness of the inner life is so restricted that they cannot effectively share no matter how willing the other person is to hear it. We see in the counseling office many people who long to have a mate who will talk to them about the details of life. Sadly, they go unfulfilled because the person simply doesn't know how to talk about the inside life. Some people have the additional problem of not connecting well to other people. They seem detached from normal life experiences most of us seek and enjoy through relationships. These people are loners and their problems go much deeper than just being unable to identify feelings. Their deepest problem is the inability to make healthy social bonds. For the person who has these deep-seated deficits, it is extremely difficult to change them in the adult years since they have to build in skills on top of an avoidant style of experiencing the world. For people more connected in relationships but unaware of their feelings, a significant amount of change can occur with patient and targeted interventions.

Fear and Shyness

All of us come into this world completely dependent upon others to help us survive. This state lasts for quite some time. All of us are capable of feeling deep fear and terror. All of us experience various forms of pain, loss, and frustration in life. Many people restrict how much they share with others because their coping mechanisms anticipate pain and disappointment. This pattern reflects the idea that it is better not to take a chance on getting hurt than it is to risk it. This person usually has experienced painful rejection or emotional neglect by key figures.

Families where children are raised with respect and interest in their life produce an adult who assumes these relationships are possible and that sharing leads to a positive payoff. Those who are criticized or judged for what they reveal learn that shame and rejection are too painful a price to pay and they anticipate that revealing themselves leads to something bad.

In a similar way, those who are raised to feel guilty when they feel something different than their parents or when they are upset with their parents often learn to inhibit expressing feelings. Many parents cannot tolerate a child's difference or the fact that they get occasionally angry with the parent. It is worth noting that this learned inhibition doesn't make the feeling go away. It simply causes confused feelings and an inability to sort out one's experiences and normal emotions.

Minimizing Problems

For many people, the idea of sharing feelings just doesn't seem relevant. Self-disclosure doesn't appear helpful or practical to these folks. The domain of emotions and expressing them to someone who cares is not an option even considered. To them, it is like having a problem with your car engine and deciding to go to college as a solution. It simply seems irrelevant.

Unfortunately, people who believe this are wrong. It is relevant to talk about feelings, particularly for women. As John Gray says in his book, *Men are from Mars, Women are from Venus*, women as a group tend to work out their stress through talking about their feelings (and some men do too). Many men don't realize that this is the thing their wives want, but instead try to solve the problem or even become critical of the problem itself. Men also need to learn to express and "work through" feelings. How?

Anger

When we are angry, we rarely want to reveal the truth about what we feel, but rather we are tempted to act it out in some way to hurt the other person. For many people anger makes them want to hide and shut down, inhibiting all forms of expression. Either way, we can learn to share in a healthy, godly way when feeling any emotion, including anger.

Dr. Dale Simpson

Chapter 16 Application

Let's look at some specific things we can do to improve our sharing and communication.

1. Make identifying and expressing the inner life an important goal for you. This inner life is the color and richness of the very fabric of life. If we do not express our feelings, we make people assume or guess things about us. By not expressing feelings we give the message that knowing us thoroughly is not a part of the relationship. Like living only on potato chips, you may not die from it but you are going to have nutritional deficits that will catch up to you and produce symptoms.

2. Commit to the importance of positive communication. We need to regularly communicate affirming statements so that when negative things come up we have a context of many more positive things to cushion what we have to say. It is the liver sandwich approach: two tasty pieces of bread with nice mayonnaise and mustard (positive comments) surrounding the slab of liver (unpleasant comments). It makes it more tolerable.

3. Consider developing the habit of saying "I feel" rather than "You make me feel."

This method gives information without blaming. Also, make requests so others don't have to read your mind. In a similar way, be sure you let others know that their sharing with you is valuable.

4. Decide to take managed risks with others. Try deepening relationships with those who appear to be relatively healthy and able to accept people. With those who cannot accept feelings, it may be best to limit how much you express to them until they are ready. People can grow and you may want to try furthering the relationship at a later date.

5. Reflect upon the communication styles in the family in which you grew up. Look at the similarities and differences of your present family. What things do you want to keep? What patterns do you want to change for the next generation? Identify one thing you can do to help the next generation's communication.

6. Consider doing a study on how Jesus communicated. Look at how Paul communicated in his letters. What can you learn from them?

7. Do you have at least a few close friends you trust with your inner life? If you do, be sure to maintain them and to thank God for this gift. If not, what could you do to begin a process that will lead to making a few close friends? Do we need these people in our lives or is this optional?

Remember, life is a long journey and communication skills are part of our survival gear. Be sure you check your backpack periodically and make additions where needed.

Chapter 17: Are You Blocking Effective Communication?

"You don't have to be a magician to turn a conversation into an argument."

- Unknown

You hear it everywhere. People say, "We don't communicate." This situation reflects the typical frustration when two people have difficulty feeling understood. Actually, what is going on is not a lack of communication, but almost always a problem in the communication process. In fact, when engaged in a relationship, one can really not eliminate communication. Isn't it true that silence can scream at a partner?

In our relationships within the family, strong emotions will be tapped and brought to the surface through a variety of ways. This strong emotion can make it difficult to see one's way through and can make it difficult to keep a steady, healthy communication. Strong emotion also makes it difficult for us to listen effectively and to stay on the course of understanding the other person. Strong emotion can trigger the fight or flight response and make us become, at the moment, self-protective and self-centered. There are a number of blocks to effective communication we must overcome in order to be what God has called us to be.

Read the following list and consider the times you have engaged in these kinds of behaviors.

Dr. Dale Simpson

Advice

Problem: Many of us assume that when a person shares feelings, we are being asked for advice and that telling people what they need to do is the primary goal of the encounter. This is rarely the case and rarely what the other person needs. In fact, most people will not ask for advice if they do not feel understood first.

Solution: Most people who want to share their pains or frustrations need someone to listen, not talk. After the person feels understood, you may ask, "Have you thought of doing..." However, advice is best used when it is asked for and after showing understanding of the person and their dilemma.

Criticism and Judgmentalism

Problem: Criticism and judgment come from strong emotions that are not managed effectively. When you feel criticized by someone, defenses usually go up and sharing goes down. This is an Olympic-sized communication killer.

Solution: If you feel these emotions beginning, decide to put your position on hold during this encounter. The most effective way to have your opinions heard is to seek to understand the other person first. As you show you desire to understand another, the discussion becomes open to the other positions.

Use of Absolute Words

Problem: Words such as "never" and "always" exaggerate, and exaggeration usually inflames emotions. Absolute words often hide the truth. Rarely does something never or always happen.

Solution: Realize that using such words will not lead to a successful resolution of our concerns. It is much better to say, "frequently I feel ignored" rather than "you never listen to me."

Using "You" Statements

Problem: Starting a sentence with "you" unless it is said in an empathic way like, "you must really feel sad," tend to be perceived as blame and marshals defensiveness from the listener. Avoid "you" statements, such as "you made us late to the dinner party."

Solution: Use "I feel" statements. These "I" statements are not selfish but offer information rather than blame. "I feel uncomfortable when we are late to a dinner party," communicates information to your listener without blaming.

Body Language

Problem: A closed or disinterested posture can communicate far more than one realizes. Researchers say that far more is communicated through intonation and body language than we realize.

Solution: Be sure when you're listening or responding to someone that you square your shoulders to them and give them reasonable eye contact. Keep your voice as even in tone as you can.

Dr. Dale Simpson

Twenty Questions

Problem: Some people confronted with an issue ask one question after another, trying to get to the facts or uncover who is to blame. This strategy does not work well and should be avoided.

Solution: (A question or two, sincerely trying to understand, that follows the acknowledgment of the person's emotion is the best strategy) Once you have heard and acknowledged the person's story, seek further understanding or clarification by asking only a question or two at a time. "You must be upset with Mrs. Johnson, your Sunday School teacher. What happened today?" would be a well-placed question after the acceptance of the emotion.

Mind Reading and Playing Psychologist

Problem: It is important to think about why people say and feel what they do, but it is usually unwise to make interpretations of motive early in the conversation. "You're just saying that to get back at me" or "you've been angry at me ever since your dad left your mother" could possibly be true statements, but quite ineffective at communicating.

Solution: Two facts need to be realized to solve this problem. First, realize that being correct about someone is not the most important thing. Also, it is crucial to know that our assumptions may not be correct. A more effective way of communicating is to ask a question such as, "I'm wondering if you are still angry with me about the past," and then listen to the answer.

Biblical Truths Spoken at the Wrong Time

Problem: Spiritual platitudes or quick religious sounding answers to strong emotions or problems trivialize the problem, and trivialize God's Word. Scripture teaches that "a timely word is healing to the bones," (Prov.16:24) and if not used carefully, one can do great damage with something that is described as a "two-edged sword." Be careful about using Scripture when you don't know what else to say to a hurting person.

Solution: First of all, realize that godly people hurt and suffer with confusion and frustration. If someone is hurting, it does not mean they are not trusting God. Establish an emotional connection with this person and "weep with those who weep." (Rom. 12:15) Job's friends were empathic the first week of his suffering when they said nothing and just grieved with him. When they started speculating after that as to the nature of this suffering and even described certain truths (God will destroy the wicked; the wicked will perish in that great awful day), they did so as his tormentors.

Busyness

Problem: Some of us use busyness as a way to keep from being emotionally connected to others. We don't spend enough time with each other doing relational things, but are off busy in our own fragmented lives.

Solution: Regularly review your life to see if your schedule is making your relationships anemic. Don't hesitate to make appointments with family members to just talk. This sharing time is important.

Defensive Reactions and an Unteachable Spirit

Problem: The fear of failure, the natural tendency to blame others, and our lack of spirituality keep us pursuing that which pleases us. Often, we just don't want to face ourselves and our weaknesses. This destroys ongoing communication when we need to face something we are doing in the relationship that is not healthy.

Solution: Decide that being teachable is a godly trait, not a sign of weakness. Practice saying these phrases, and say them frequently: "I see what you mean." "I didn't know that." "I was wrong."

Stories

Problem: Every generation relates from their own perspective and explains how it was in that time period. "When I was a kid, I walked five miles through the snow." This will not necessarily solve a problem for the next generation.

Solution: Discipline your thinking, realizing that such illustrations will **rarely** benefit your children. Stay focused on the emotional component of their stories or problems and connect to that. If you can remember how it felt to be in a similar situation, use that to build more empathy for your child and express that to him.

Talking Too Much About Ourselves

Problem: Often when someone shares something in a conversation, the other person says something like "Oh yeah, I felt that way" and they tell you their experience. Taking the attention off the other person and drawing it back onto us is a communication stopper, especially if it is right after an initial sharing.

Solution: Stay focused on the other person's experiences. Make (at least three) statements or questions about what this person said before you share your experience. "It sounds like you had a good time." "Was that your first-time skiing?" "Boy, I bet you want to go back soon."

Improving your communication may require effort to stop yourself from saying the wrong thing and plugging in something better. Whatever you end up saying, work hard to first communicate understanding of the other person before running off on another idea. Giving the gift of understanding is more profound than most of us realize. It connects you to the heart of the other person and places the importance of a transaction right where God himself places it: on the relationship.

Take time now to commit to changing one thing in your communication to make it more person oriented and less problem oriented. Tell someone in the family what you are working on and ask them to watch for changes. Mutual accountability will help you back up the desire to change.

Chapter 17 Application

1. Why isn't advice usually helpful?

2. Does a person feel differently about truth discovered vs. truth told to them in advice?

3. Can you put your need to fix or help another person on hold long enough to understand them? How will this make you more or less effective in relationships?

4. Would you commit to cutting out words like never and always? What would help you catch yourself?

5. If people process emotions differently, how can this knowledge help you with others?

Homeschooling for Life

Section 4: Homeschooling and Life

Chapter 18: Is Giftedness Next to Godliness?

"Originality is simply a pair of fresh eyes."

- Thomas Higginson

Attention please. All gifted Christians, please go to Room A. All others go to Room B. Once in your respective rooms, all talented people sit in the front of the room, and the rest please sit at the rear.

Now, ask yourself, does it feel the same in each room and in each position. Would you feel uncomfortable if you were in the untalented, ungifted group? What if you knew your parents and other adults had their car bumpers plastered with stickers reading "I'm the proud parent of a gifted, talented student," referring to your sibling.

These are some of the questions not asked in our culture's quest for success and excellence. In an attempt to be helpful, culture starts a labeling process that divides. This tendency to segment people into categories, usually reflecting good vs. bad, is at best an attempt to organize our world and at worst, a desire to construct esteem from certain attributes. We in homeschooling should think through this process which polarizes along intellectual lines.

Of course, most people use the terms gifted and talented as a way to categorize, not as a way to put others down. Parents, teachers, and administrators try to acknowledge certain abilities and encourage their students with those standout abilities. They focus on encouraging certain students rather than discouraging other students. But an educational climate that categorizes on giftedness is making a loud statement to all children and parents regarding values and worth. So, what then do we do with children who appear especially able in abstract thinking and traditional intellectual abilities? Clearly these children exist, and ignoring their distinctiveness will not necessarily help them or other children of lesser abilities. To come to a reasoned, Christian, educational perspective on this subject, let's look for a moment at how giftedness has traditionally been defined.

Giftedness traditionally is determined based upon intelligence test scores of 130 or above. This cut-off (two standard deviations above the mean) was arbitrarily chosen and it reflects children in the upper 3%-4% of the population on what the test measures. For years, intelligence tests have been criticized for being culture-bound and tending to measure values and understanding of a particular culture rather than raw, innate intelligence. There is some merit to these arguments. What we CAN say about IQ scores is that they tend to indicate chance of success in formal higher education (though this is in no way a large correlation). Some school systems, seeing the weakness of using IQ scores only, have included additional indicators of giftedness and talent, such as abilities in the arts, leadership, and initiative.

Interestingly, when this additional set of criteria was proposed in a local school district, the parents of gifted and talented kids were irate, saying that using other criteria was watering down the intellectual standard (and, presumably, the elite character) of the class.

Frequently, we see parents using the gifted and talented designation as a statement about their child to the world. People have agonized over a child's failure to make it into the elite class. I believe this missed the point and reflects on the parental needs to feel significant through their children. This loss of perspective can occur just as easily in homeschooling families if we are too emotionally invested in our children being advanced and of superior performance.

The purpose of labeling gifted and talented students is to accommodate their higher abilities by providing educational experiences that match or utilize those abilities. We want to maximize their learning while getting the most out of our educational dollar. Kids labeled gifted and talented frequently flounder in the standard classroom, where they become bored, restless, and sometimes refuse to do work, seemingly as a protest to what feels to them as a prison sentence of uninteresting classes. In my practice, I have worked with kids who were advanced in intellectual abilities and failing in the classroom. These kids often feel isolated, lonely, and under-motivated.

What is the typical school response to kids labeled gifted and talented? My experience has shown that the gifted classes tend to be less structured and include more learning by doing. Students act out plays, publish a newspaper, write stories, plan how to run government, etc. It appears that schools are trying to reverse the "dumbing down" of the average classroom which tends to teach to the lowest common denominator, thereby losing the kids ready for more of a challenge.

Of course, as a home schooler, I can see that the schools are trying to recapture the ability to individualize instruction based upon the uniqueness of each student. Interestingly, this is the very philosophy that the homeschooling movement champions. Every learner deserves to be taught at his level using methods that are matched to his learning style. Gifted and talented classes consisting of good, creative, individualized instruction should be provided for all children.

Homeschooling provides an environment where individual needs and differences can be respected and fulfilled. Gone is the need to categorize and polarize students into the smart-dumb or talented-untalented groups. In homeschooling, we not only have the concept of individual instruction, but we have the means to accomplish it. Consider the Christian perspective.

First, throughout Scripture, wisdom is preferred above intelligence. The ability to exercise the will in making a godly choice when faced with a decision is valued more than gold (Prov. 3:13-14; Ps. 9:10). It is easy for secular man to overvalue intelligence since it reflects human understanding and the power of the mind to organize information. Intelligence, logic, and analysis are wonderful aspects of the human nature created by God. They even reflect some of the characteristics of God. But God warns us not to "... lean on (our) own understanding" (Prov. 3:5). Self-control that exercises godly choices is more valuable.

Second, Ephesians teaches that there is great diversity within the Christian community — diversity that is necessary and designed by God. All God's people have gifts and talents to be used to build up the Christian community and to participate in the kingdom. Intellectual abilities are just one of the countless traits, skills, and talents useful to the church. The ability to express kindness, perseverance, and self-control are at least as important as IQ scores. Students who are concrete thinkers, who may want to repair small engines, are not to be valued any less than youngsters who enter college at seventeen. Christian teachers and parents must be careful to ask, "What am I communicating about the importance of various abilities and skills? Does the giftedness designation imply extra worth?"

Third, a student who seems beyond his years in abstract thinking and intellect is still a kid who must learn about emotions, relationships, and choices. We must not miss meeting the nonintellectual needs of children because we overestimate their functioning based upon cognitive advancement. Kids with high IQ's can easily be shaped into the success track and eventually become the burned-out intellectuals of tomorrow. Teaching a balanced life is necessary. Real life is more than being a card-carrying member of MENSA (an international organization for individuals with a high IQ).

Fourth, when making a distinction based upon performance, the designation "honors" class or "honors" student may be an improvement to gifted and talented. Honors suggests a level of achievement, whereas gifted and talented suggest innate ability and value. As with outward beauty, we want to be careful not to overvalue temporal, materialistic qualities.

As home schoolers, we have the ability to give enriched, individual instruction. Of course, during busy weeks, we are happy just to get the minimal daily educational requirements done, much less provide advanced experiences. Yet the home school alternative allows us to treat the gifts and talents in all our students with dignity and care. Next time you categorize kids into giftedness and non-giftedness, consider the big picture. Try to meet the student's educational needs without using polarizing labels and groupings. Our kids deserve it...all of them.

Chapter 18 Application

1. Do you see your family members as people with various gifts and abilities? Is there someone labeled "gifted" in the family? How might children feel if they were or were not labeled gifted? How can you help develop the gifts and abilities in each child? Pick one ability in each child to strengthen in the next six months.

2. Are skills of abstract reasoning and general creativity the most valued of skills in life? Why or why not?

3. What non-school abilities are you developing in yourself and in your children?

4. If your children achieve high IQ scores or high academic honors, what does that say about you?

Chapter 19: Homeschooling in the Real World

"Reading and writing, arithmetic and grammar do not constitute education, any more than a knife, fork and spoon constitute a dinner."

- Lubbock

23 minutes into the school year, Christine flushed her school schedule down the toilet.

When you read an article, book, or attend a seminar, do you ever respond to the author or speaker with, "She's amazing! How can she clean house, write four books a year, bake bread every week, till a half-acre garden, and manage her eight children (all of whom she delivered naturally at home), and I can't even do my own job around the house, much less teach my two children?" If you're a new home schooler, you may not have thought this yet, but get ready...you will.

Dr. Dale Simpson

Could some people quit homeschooling due to the images they have of what constitutes a good home schooler? Could it be that teachers have expectations that are based upon something other than reality, and when reality hits, they become discouraged?

So many times, we put writers, leaders, and nationally known figures on a pedestal. Our images of them often serve as our models. We will probably think of half the home schoolers in our support group as doing far better in life management than we are. Yet we are all in different life stages and different circumstances, defying simple comparisons.

The media uses a technique called air brushing, which makes people look better than they are. Why? Value is in appearances...looking right...thinking right...acting right. Gorgeous women and handsome men and perfect families, something most of us are not, produce dissatisfaction with ourselves. It causes us to strive for an unrealistic ideal.

Perfectionism and rigidity can be found throughout the home school movement, sometimes coming down from home school leaders. Many women labor under their own problems with perfectionism and never feel like they've achieved what they ought. They are easily trapped into condemnation by these problems. St. Paul anticipated this when he wrote that we should not let the traditions and ideas of men steal our freedom (Gal. 5:1; Col. 3:20).

Don't be fooled by appearances of everyone having it together. EVERYONE DOESN'T HAVE IT TOGETHER. Perfection doesn't exist on earth.

You don't have to be Wonder Woman to home school effectively. You don't have to be a compulsive over-achiever to please God.

Lifestyle management choices must be made. No one can do everything, and thankfully, God doesn't require you to do everything.

You can be reasonably sure that you'll have days wishing you'd never even thought of homeschooling. You may feel all alone. This isolation happens because we are not honest with each other about our lives.

Here's an admonition for new home schoolers: Churches see you as a stay-at-home parent and may expect you to volunteer for them because you have "free time." If you recently left a job outside the home, your spouse could see you as having "stopped work." Yet you have traded one job for another. This can cause burn-out quickly. "No" sometimes must be said to worthwhile projects and efforts in order to protect the priorities for the home school family.

Also, homeschooling is a full-time teaching job, and harder in some respects than the traditional classroom because a) you can't use last year's lesson plans as much, b) you don't punch out at 3:00 p.m., c) you don't have the structure of classes changing every 45 minutes, and you have many hats to wear with your students because they are your children. These should be acknowledged and adjusted to accordingly.

Be sure to plan for set-back days. Give yourself room to take a day off and go to the park. Flex days with no work and no school must be okay. You don't have to do every page in a workbook. You don't have to do every lesson in a book. Too many teachers find peace only when they do everything the textbooks tell them to do, (They are set-up for failure.)

Some parents may feel their child's success in school is a reflection upon them, and to some degree it is. But a parent's sense of value can get linked to outward academic success in a child, causing her anxiety which gets translated into undue pressure on the child. Parents need to be encouraged in the process of learning, the love of learning, and growth within the individual child. Learning takes place in different settings and different formats, not just with a text book. Look for the learning in places you least expect it. Don't settle for a narrow view that learning is what happens in formal education.

Let's not pass perfectionism on to our children. Give yourself and your children room to fail. Give lots of room.

Be careful with what you read and hear by leaders in the field. Scrutinize this chapter, this book, and other writings. Is someone expounding on a biblical principle, or are they establishing a principle based on their logic and making it dogma? Adding our own spin to Scripture is dangerous when taught as "thus saith the Lord." The models for behavior must be reasonable ones found in an honest Christian perspective.

Be careful about oversimplifying life with spiritual clichés and platitudes. Remember Job's friends who went from being helpful in their silence to tormenting poor Job when, among other things, they used scriptural truths inappropriately. Be careful with each other and with Scripture. You can hurt or discourage with Scripture (a sword can protect or hurt).

Let's project realistic images to each other. Let's be honest about the real stuff of homeschooling and life. Then, maybe, we can see the fruits of our efforts in fewer dropouts and less stress for all of us.

Homeschooling in Hollywood

Why is the drop-out rate noticeable in homeschooling if it's such a great thing? Part of the answer lies in the Hollywood Syndrome, the atmosphere where things appear real but often aren't. The town looks real but actually has nothing behind it; the actress looks beautiful but behind her make-up and hairpieces, she is less than glamorous. Perhaps our models and expectations of homeschooling are unrealistic.

Previously, we looked at the distortions brought about by anxiety, insecurity, and perfectionism. We saw how home educating parents often are trapped by the need to do everything right, to do every page in a workbook, to become driven even by some leaders in the movement, to never be satisfied with one's performance. Let's consider four more aspects of real homeschooling that, in my opinion, need to be understood for survival in the real world.

To begin with, you don't have to adopt the old educational ways. Good homeschooling is not just adopting the philosophy or method of traditional education found in public or private schools. We have the freedom to have an educational philosophy that is not based on what is easiest for the bureaucracy, which is so often the case in traditional classrooms.

Moreover, we have the freedom to teach the individual, not the curriculum. Yet so much of the old thinking is in our heads, especially with new home schoolers. People still think there is something written in stone that says all fourth graders must learn x, y, and z, not realizing how arbitrary and limiting this is. Homeschooling should give us the freedom to look at these lists as interesting, but not as law. Learning happens all the time and not primarily in the schoolroom. We learn in the context of meaningful activities. Realistic home education understands and values this truth instead of believing that education lives only in textbooks.

Perhaps, even more importantly, we are teaching not only academics at home, but also how to deal with challenges of life by how we structure our lives and by the things we do. We are teaching how to manage time, how to handle frustrations, how to practice self-control, how to complete tasks in a reasonable way, and how to have fun. Don't be afraid if you are having a particularly difficult day, and nobody seems to want to learn, and nobody is getting along with each other, and you are exhausted. Close the books, head to the park, or head to your bedroom with a good novel. You don't have to have over-achieving kids to be a good home schooler.

Always keep in mind that real homeschooling is diverse. Real homeschooling is about real thoughts and real feelings. We can think freely for there is not only one correct way to think or do things. I see in some circles a growing political and religious correctness in appearance and thinking. We must not let this get in the way of living the particular way God has called us to live. Real homeschooling is primarily of the heart, not the head, nor a political party, nor a "right" set of thoughts. There is no need for someone to put the stamp of approval on materials or books or curriculum or the way to think. Too often, people seek security in an uncertain world by simply adopting a party line and then leave their thinking at the door.

In the Christian world, we can say our curriculum or philosophy is biblical, and it will sell just because of our claim. But what do these claims mean? Can we study and enjoy a secular writer or artist and not be criticized as being worldly? Is everything God would have us learn contained in the Scriptures? If it were, we would go to theologians for car repairs or for brain surgery. I am continually amazed at what isn't in the Bible. God permits "taking from the Egyptians" as one popular writer says.

It is also good to remember that real homeschooling is developmental. As teachers, we are to be knowledgeable about the particular stage of emotional and intellectual life of our children. We don't treat them like little adults. The Bible is full of developmental examples.

"I gave you milk, not solid food, for you were not yet ready for it."
1 Cor. 3:2

"... You need milk, not solid food... solid food is for the mature..."
Heb. 5: 12-14

"Like newborn babies, crave pure spiritual milk, so that by it you may grow up..." 1 Pet. 2:2

"When I was a child, I talked like a child, I thought like a child, I reasoned like a child. When I became a man, I put childish ways behind me." 1 Cor. 13:11

Developmental thinking means we learn our children's styles. It means believing in the readiness concept, the thing that tells us not to toilet train youngsters before their muscles have matured. Children need time to interact with the world and mature cognitively and emotionally so they can effectively process life.

Real homeschooling helps develop the choosing, thinking child while parents serve as guide to the child. It helps the child make choices early, helps him learn effective ways of living, and it helps him develop wisdom. Following authority figures blindly can ruin a person, especially in a world increasingly hostile to Christianity. Following an individual Christian leader is unwise and a throwback to the Old Testament example of the people of Ancient Israel demanding a king.

And finally, real homeschooling also includes a marriage. Simply put, our marriages must be maintained within the home educating family. This is one of two visible relationships that serve as home base to kids (the other being the parent-child relationship). It provides security to children or in the case of poor marriages, it can rob them of the safety needed to grow. Your children will pick up on the stresses and strains in your marriage. You cannot totally hide the tensions between parents. The only solution is to deal with the stresses and work with your mate in an honest way to deal with the pain of growing together.

Homeschooling can increase the stress on a marriage and therefore it must be handled with increased communication between partners. A frequent problem occurs when the husband gets frustrated because mom has lesson planning to do, and he wants more time with her. Another marital problem that can arise is when the dad questions mom because the kids aren't appearing to achieve academically like other kids he knows or hears about. This can drive the mom further into insecurity and, if not handled well as a couple, can lead to serious conflict. Just as a reminder, in today's society, it is quite possible for the roles to be reversed.

To make sure you home school in reality and not in Hollywood, set up a minimum of one time each week to discuss family life, scheduling, school progress, individual needs, and the workload in the home. Moms and dads, be sure to ask for help before you're in a crisis. Also keep a date night in your schedule and don't discuss problems there.

Real homeschooling involves personal stewardship. So often we only think of stewardship in terms of godly management of money. But stewardship involves the godly management of any asset placed in our lives. Being a good steward of the life given to us means taking care of ourselves physically, spiritually, emotionally, and intellectually. A mom's ability to nurture others while putting her needs on hold (a wonderful ability) can so dominate some women that mom may think she does not "have time" for self-care. Some people can more easily give regular maintenance to their car than to themselves. The real homeschooling family must give great latitude and encouragement for mom to enjoy taking time for herself with a clear conscience.

Unfortunately, many homeschooling women are often not good at this. But the airbrushed versions of the perfect mom who gives and keeps on going endlessly like the battery powered bunny on TV are simply not real. Mom's time must be protected. Some delegation of tasks is necessary.

If possible, hire someone to clean one day a week or month. Spend a few dollars doing something for yourself. Let someone help when you have pressing things that only you can do.

There will likely be days even in the best home school families when the kids don't want to be home schooled. Likewise, there will be days when you don't want to teach them anymore. These feelings are quite common and can be worked through. We can realize that life tends to cycle.

There is hope. For new home educators, things will get better after the first one or two years. It becomes easier to understand the learning styles of your children, easier to figure out curriculum you want and curriculum that doesn't work.

Have fun. Honestly deal with life. Don't look at Hollywood. It's not real.

Chapter 19 Application

1. Have you ever wrestled with perfectionism in yourself or in others around you?

2. Do you ever see an "airbrushed" or "Photoshopped" image projected in the world around you? When have you recognized your home school or church group being honest or putting on airs?

3. How can you be genuine without losing the ability to be encouraging?

4. Have you ever felt guilty because you weren't like someone you see in books, magazines, or behind the podium? How can you manage this?

5. Should homeschooling be about the business of copying traditional education? Should it be focusing upon being better than traditional education? Should it be student or curriculum oriented?

6. How can homeschoolers help each other avoid the Hollywood trap?

Dr. Dale Simpson

Chapter 20: Are Your Standards Hurting You?

It was a common problem for homeschooling moms, but Mabel had set the standard way too high.

Most homeschooling moms are committed to give what it takes of themselves to properly nurture and train their children. The sacrificial heart found in mothers enables them to go from one activity to another, sometimes managing two or three at a time, all in the service of others. Feeling the central responsibility for the emotional and educational life of the family becomes routine, as does her ability to put her own needs on hold for the higher good. A mother's ability to look to others' needs rather than her own provides vital ministry to the family and models selflessness to the children.

Accompanying this busy, giving lifestyle is the tendency for moms to assume they are not doing enough, especially when comparing themselves to friends or to their image of what others are doing. Magazine articles and books are often discouraging because they suggest more and more things to accomplish, which can be interpreted as additional tasks she should be accomplishing. Portrayals of successful homeschooling families frequently seem to be as perfect as the well-kept living room pictured in women's magazines, making moms feel more insecure. So many women find themselves trapped in the "I'm not doing enough" syndrome. They become disheartened because the spilled Cheerios were stuck all day on the kitchen table and they failed to bake bread or teach math that day.

Thoughts of running away, giving up all responsibility, and sending the kids off to traditional school only serve to make teaching moms feel guiltier. This often drives them to more work in order to compensate. Fears of not accomplishing academic goals increase as the teacher gives more and more of herself to the tasks. If this process continues, burn-out results. Many home schoolers have quit, saying that homeschooling was overwhelming.

Like so many other things, the virtue of selfless giving, if not balanced by replenishing, lead to problems. The Bible gives many examples, including God resting after creation (He wasn't tired, He was contemplating and enjoying what He had made), Jesus getting away by Himself on many occasions, and the message of Ecclesiastes 3, which encourages the timely balance of all areas of life. Clearly, we need an understanding of the need for relaxation if we are to pursue our God-given call to home school.

Understanding the need for relaxation or recharging is a matter of applying the model of stewardship to our lives. Rather than looking out for ourselves, we are to look out for what is valuable to God, including our emotional lives. By maintaining ourselves properly, we will have the stamina and clear thinking to persevere to the end. Shoddy maintenance may save money and time in the short run. The trouble is that we are not in a sprint but rather in a marathon. Our ultimate goal is not to work harder, nor is it to complete a particularly complex curriculum. Our task is not to do everything that can be done. Excellence is not compulsiveness. If it were, Jesus would not have had such disagreement with the ways of the Pharisees.

What can be done to keep proper balance and stay on course? First, review your expectations. Are you trying to imitate the traditional classroom? Have you slipped into the methods you came to homeschooling to avoid? Unrealistic expectations, like a stone thrown into a smooth pond, will cause ripples of stress to hit all sides (and all people in your family). Try to be more flexible. The thing you think has to be done today probably can be put off until you have more time.

Second, ask yourself if you are driven, and if so, what drives you? Is there a guilt-ridden person inside trying to prove something to extended family members in order to win them over to homeschooling? These issues must be faced if we are to live less stressfully.

Third, realize when you say "yes" to something, you are saying "no" to something else. The inability to say "no" to certain good things that come your way will create more stress. You shouldn't be doing every good thing but the good things that are the current priorities in your life.

Fourth, talk with others about the standards they are realistically meeting. Don't assume that others are doing more than you in their homeschooling.

Fifth, plan regular time during the day and week for reflection and enjoyment. Ask your husband to help protect the time you want and need.

Sixth, review the three broad areas of curriculum, family scheduling, and teaching methods. Are there times or methods that are more stressful than others? Can you, for example, teach more on Monday when you are geared up and teach less on Friday when you are tired from the demands of the week? Also ask yourself, "Are there things I can delegate to someone else, or even eliminate that keep me from doing the truly necessary things?"

A seventh point to ponder is found in an experience I had last year. A new home schooler visited our home and as I apologized for the untidiness, he said, "Hey…I'm glad you are this way…I feel safe and don't have to pretend." Resolve to never appear so together that others are unable to be themselves. Be real and communicate encouragement and truth to others.

A last point is this: when others seem to be so effective, having well-washed, perfectly mannered kids, and running a business on the side, don't be fooled. Other information may be missing from the picture. As the adage goes, "If it looks too good to be true, it probably is." Let God give you peace where you are, rather than chronically feeling inadequate around others.

Resolve now to allow yourself to do things like play more, laugh more, loosen up, soak in your bathtub, read a novel, or adapt a schedule. Then maybe you will be able to continue to do your best.

As Thomas Fuller said in the 1600's, "Contentment consists not in adding more fuel but in taking away some fire."

Chapter 20 Application

1. Discuss the reasons you home school and your expectations and hopes for outcomes.

2. Discuss where you fall on the continuum of driven and hard working to laid back and passive. What are the strengths and weaknesses of your position?

3. Are you a hard worker, driven by fears of something? What could that something be?

4. Can you say "no" to your spouse and your children? Your parents? People in your church? Is there anyone in your life with whom you do not feel as free to be balanced in your relationship between giving and self-care? What would you need to do to change and make it a less lop-sided relationship?

5. Some people grow up so trained to meet the needs of others that they do not know their own perspective. They are somewhat invisible or chameleon like. Do you know how to identify what you like in food, clothes, interests, etc.? Commit to doing one thing in the next

few days just because you enjoy it. Monitor your thinking to see if you hear messages in your head that tell you that you shouldn't.

6. Discuss your family of origin's view on recreation. Discuss your view.

7. Can you give structure and a schedule to your daily life or do you tend to react?

Could stress build in your life because of insufficient planning and constantly running late?

Is there a pattern of self-indulgence that creates problems and hurts your personal stewardship and self-care?

What is one thing you could change to improve your way of life?

8. How well do you shift when something interrupts your schedule? Are your activities spaced properly to prepare for sick children and unplanned events, or are they stacked so closely that normal life is frustrating everything you are doing?

Dr. Dale Simpson

Chapter 21: Balancing the Roles of Teacher and Parent

"Much study is weariness to the bones and the writing of books is endless."

- Solomon, Ecclesiastes 12:12

Home schoolers, as formal teachers, wear an additional hat to that of parent and authority. Teaching parents have an additional responsibility to plan and execute a learning process that will prepare their children for the rigors of life. The parent must create an environment that focuses on learning and organizes it so that important life lessons can be acquired. Tension can result from the dual roles of parent and teacher, student and child.

Let's look at some practical ways to balance roles and maintain home order in the home school.

1. Parents need to establish school rules and expectations. Many families establish a place, room, even a table, where focused learning takes place. Home schoolers are aware that all of life is learning, and focused learning is what we accomplish through our teaching. This requires a bit of structure to make it happen. For example, school time may require a somewhat different set of rules than general family living. For instance, the rule that you don't interrupt mom when she is teaching others unless it is an emergency may be a stiffer one than during non-school time. Similarly, a system for small offenses may be applied in the school setting and not at other times. Just as a game with no rules would

be impossible to play, structured learning requires rules and expectations to guide the process and give it meaning.

2. Home educators need to take a hard look at how comfortable they are with their own authority and inter-personal power. Parents vary along a continuum, from those who are uncomfortable with their strength to those who seek to dominate and control. Healthy parenting and teaching involve a comfort with one's authority without the need to prove it. Overly dominant or controlling parents can lead to the same pattern in a child or, in reaction, a person uncomfortable with his personal power. Passivity in parenting can lead some children to develop a self-indulgent style that doesn't say "no" to itself. Passive parenting styles also can give rise to lack of initiative on the children's part. You may be the parent who can watch a child dismantle a living room before you think to intervene. Many parents uncomfortable with their personal power tend to be their children's buddies and also over explain. These adults try to reason with a child as if the child has to agree with the parent's decision before the parent can move ahead. Parents need to learn to give simple explanations or simple consequences if it is in a discipline context and leave it at that.

Reasonable and appropriate consequences applied with compassion and nurturing will teach children self-control without undue hostility to the parent. When Mary is failing to do her work and day dreaming during school about the fun she will have at her friend's house that night, a parent might say, "Hey, I know you've a good deal on your mind. You can do the rest of this work at another time. You just need to have it completed before you go to Martha's. Perhaps working in the yard is something you could do now." This is far better than nagging since it lets her sweat over the consequences and the turf is something you can control. Note that we control ourselves and the environment, NOT THE CHILD. The control of the child rests with her, which is where we want it.

3. The educating parent's role can be helped by being a genuine person and letting children experience us in a deep way. Genuineness occurs when we avoid putting on an image around those inside as well as outside the family. Children become disillusioned and lose respect for us when they see superficial impression-making in the parent. Genuine living requires us to lay aside the maneuvering that has those watching our lives looking at the illusion instead of the real article. A transparency and openness will build trust and respect.

Allow your children to have different opinions and feelings without judging them. As unique individuals, children will perceive and feel in a variety of ways, often in contrast to you. Do not question their spirituality, loyalty or respect if they are different. Just acknowledge their perspective, and if you think some redirection is needed, present your points in a respectful way.

Healthy day to day interaction deepens the relationships you can have with your children, and it helps in the shifting roles one must play. How we handle personal wrongs and painful experiences support or detract from our authority. Apologizing and asking for forgiveness is not only morally correct, but wise leadership. Using the "confess, repent and ask for forgiveness" model will score big points with your children. Confessing is a simple statement of what we did wrong without any excuses. "I should not have yelled at you," would be adequate. Next, the repenting phase calls us to commit to change, saying, "I need to handle my anger in a better way and will work on it." The final part simply has the offender ask, "Would you forgive me?" Use this regularly, and have your little charges walk through the three steps when they offend, and you will see great benefits.

One helpful way to balance the parent-teacher role is to share with your child a time you struggled with something personal and how you made it through. This genuineness, when done in appropriate amounts, can strengthen the parents' authority. Teaching parents need to say, "I don't know," if they don't know. One should not feel fearful if you are ignorant of an answer, but use the occasion to show what to do when you don't know. Maybe you could find the answer together. Good authority doesn't mean you have to know everything or that you make no mistakes.

4. Spouse support is critical to the establishment of the teacher role for the parent. Children need to see both parents endorse the home school experience. Any indifference or undercutting by the nonteaching parent will be perceived by the child, reducing the student's cooperation. The nonteaching parent can take an interest in academics so there are two parents associated with the need to keep up with schoolwork. Taking the parenting burden off the teaching parent during the evenings and weekends is important and helpful. Making provisions for the teaching spouse to experience fun things is advisable. A husband needs to occasionally suggest to his wife to take time for herself, while he takes care of the children.

The teaching parent should be seen as a working parent with a serious, and for the most part, full time job. The job is much more than the actual teaching. It is preparation, planning, curriculum selection and updating curriculum, ad infinitum. Parents who are not appreciated for the many hats they wear will struggle more in their roles, often resenting certain responsibilities. A spouse needs to say, "You are doing a great job, and I appreciate the effort you give to our children's education." Remember, she doesn't get a paycheck like some teachers.

If you are a homeschooling parent with no support from a spouse, be sure to involve yourself with other teaching parents in your local support group. You must build in regular contact to keep your sanity and drink in encouragement to keep going. Monthly lunch meetings and trading child care among other parents can be emotional lifesavers. Ask a few home school veterans if you can call them just for brief encouragement when things get to you. We all have those days where we doubt our effectiveness, and simple contact from a fellow traveler on the road can be a cup of cold water to a thirsty soul (Prov. 25:25).

5. Finally, playing the role of parent, teacher, principal and curriculum consultant can lead to fatigue and burnout. This is, of course, a risk for all of us in this crazy, fragmented, overly busy society. Home schoolers have their special vulnerabilities to this. Be sure to develop an atmosphere that values taking care of the teacher as an act of good stewardship and long-range maintenance of the life God has given us. The principle of rest and reflection is an established one since God created the world.

Don't try to do everything each day. Give yourself permission to take a day off if things seem as though they are falling apart. The teaching parent usually fills her days in the home or in the family car. This leads to environment fatigue and boredom. The educating parent needs weekly or biweekly relief outside the daily atmosphere for a short while.

6. Give yourself time to learn and enough room to make mistakes. Remind yourself that excellence is not perfectionism. God is as concerned about the process of how we arrive at our destination as the destination itself. Excellence is doing what God has called you to do with the resources you have. It is not comparing outcomes. Avoid naive comparisons of your teaching style with that of others. A mom with three specials needs children should count success in different ways than a teacher with one child who excels with traditional curriculum. A single parent who is homeschooling should guard herself from feeling inadequate

because she isn't doing the same educational activities other families are able to do. If God has led you to homeschooling, He will help you find your style and the methods that work best for your particular situation and your particular children.

7. One way to counteract the fragmentation of modern life and to bring more cohesion into the family is to use the family council technique.

The purpose for the council is to exchange important information, support the members, aid in problem solving, and support family order. Family projects and outings can be planned as a group. Conflicts can be resolved. People can be praised. Members may decide to save or earn additional money for a trip or for supporting a missionary. The possibilities are limited only by the family's desire and vision.

The rules for family councils are simple. First, everyone speaks for themselves and respects others' rights to their opinion. Second, a chairperson is appointed and runs each meeting by keeping things on track. The chair is rotated each meeting so everyone gets a turn. Third, there is a secretary to record any business that needs to be tracked to a later conclusion (usually by the next meeting). Fourth, each person speaks without others interrupting. Meetings can begin with a prayer, discussion of old business (if any), and then opening the floor for new business.

The day of the first family council should find a parent (I recommend the dad) leading by introducing the rules and explaining the purpose of the council. This meeting should be kept to ten minutes or less to set the expectation for brief assemblies. Since there is no old business the first meeting, I suggest parents have a task they would like the family to accomplish (e.g. each person saying one thing they like about other members, or state three things by which you'd like to be remembered). The first family council in particular and all of them in general should primarily be for pointing out positive things and expressing feelings rather than focusing upon criticism. The council can be a regular opportunity to point out to each child evidence of desired character traits that parents see developing. One of the common mistakes of families is to use the meetings as a time for the parents to gang up on kids. We do not want to set an us (parents) against them (kids) tone but rather identify as a group of individuals who must work together to accomplish life tasks and solve problems.

For some parents this will sound like one person, one vote, or some tangled method of empowering children with just as much family power as the parents. This is not the case. Parents always have the responsibility to help structure family interaction and maintain a godly direction for the group. Communicating openly while working together to solve problems that affect everyone is not antagonistic to a proper structural hierarchy of family decision making. In fact, as I have argued strongly in other writings, we must facilitate and enhance our children's expressions of the inner life. This is not self-preoccupation, as some have criticized. It is wise management of our lives. What you can identify inside can be appraised and controlled with God's help. The hidden things deep within the human heart, the Bible says, are often the things that deceive and control us. The wisest form of leadership is one that provides those being led the ability to express themselves and be heard. This, after all, is what God does for us.

The council is also a great way to teach how a business meeting is run. It helps children understand there is a process and procedure to solving problems in a group. These skills will be needed in the workplace or in their future family life.

Conflict that arises between siblings can tire the hard-working parent who is often asked to be judge and jury. The offended child may come whining to the parent saying, "Look what Johnny did...you have to do something." This matter could be handled by the parents or it could be referred to the family council. Children can come up with great ideas we adults often miss. When assigning consequences for siblings' misbehavior, they are learning something in the process and developing family cohesion and organization. When siblings participate in settling a consequence for one another, it not only teaches them the process but it also helps dissipate their hurt or anger if they have been offended. Perhaps this is why the Old Testament tends to involve those offended in the meeting. Justice was not carried out by far removed, unaffected people but rather by the parties or families who suffered the loss.

Misbehavior that is discussed in a group will tend to be spotted by others more easily than misbehavior seen only by one other person. Group pressure can exert influence. Problem behavior more easily flourishes when hidden and withers in the light of public examination.

Family councils can be held at a preset time (say, after lunch on Sunday) or they can be called spontaneously to deal with an issue. When I worked in a residential therapy program, we called the unplanned ones "huddle up" and they were used effectively to deal with a conflict at the time it happened. Whatever your family does, I encourage you to consider this method of family involvement, especially as children grow older and are spending more time outside the home.

The dual roles of teacher and parent can be challenging for the homeschooling mom or dad. With a relaxed attitude, support from other parents, and a Christian perspective on success, families who educate at home can reach the goals they seek.

Chapter 21 Application

1. What is your comfort level as a parent? As a teacher?

2. Is it difficult for your child to know when you are in your teacher role? If so, how can you shift roles more clearly?

3. In what ways could you use the Family Council meeting? What are two things to remember when carrying out this meeting?

ISBN 978-0-9988624-3-9

Dr. Dale Simpson

Other family resources available through Learning for Life Press

The Easy to Make Paper Airplane Book by Lane Simpson
Your children's fun will take off while they learn the basics of flight from this easy-to-use book. All designs have step-by-step instructions tested by children worldwide. All your children need is notebook paper and off they go!

Web site: www.learningforlifepress.com
Get your copy today at Amazon
ISBN 978-0-9988624-0-8

A Study in Wisdom by Dr. Dale Simpson

This highly effective study for children ages 5 to 12 focuses upon the importance of wise choices in life while also teaching empathy, thinking skills, and communication. After a 6-week study of verses from Proverbs, any Bible storybook can help children apply their knowledge of wisdom to choices in their daily lives. This parent led study requires no preparation, no knowledge of the Bible, engages children in conversation and activities, and has many activity sheets that can be photocopied and used with multiple children. This resource is great for anyone

Homeschooling for Life

raising young children with a theistic (belief in one personal God); it is particularly beneficial for Jewish or Christian families.

Get free children's picture Bible along with other free resources at our website: www.learningforlifepress.com

Get your copy today at Amazon
ISBN 978-0-9988624-5-3

Think It, Feel It, Say It! Board Game

Do you want your family to learn about others, communicate better, and practice making wise choices while having tons of fun? The Think It, Feel It, Say It! game is just what you need. Enjoy the discussions, the laughs, and the wonderful interactions. Your children and your family will grow together!

The colorful and engaging game combines fun with self-expression, identifying feelings, thinking through difficult encounters, learning wisdom, and gaining self-confidence.

Dr. Dale Simpson

Parents and children will deepen their knowledge of each other and make fun memories at the same time.

Ages: 6 – Above
Players: 2 – 8

The Think It, Feel It, Say It! Board Game is available for purchase through www.learningforlifepress.com

Visit us for our free newsletter, downloads and resources.
Email: info@learningforlifepress.com

www.ingramcontent.com/pod-product-compliance
Lightning Source LLC
Chambersburg PA
CBHW070546010526
44118CB00012B/1245